TEACHING LIBRARY SKILLS IN GRADES K THROUGH 6

A How-To-Do-It Manual

CATHARYN ROACH
JOANNE MOORE

HOW-TO-DO-IT MANUALS FOR SCHOOL AND PUBLIC LIBRARIANS
Number 10

Series Editor: Barbara L. Stein

D1441673

NEAL-SCHUMAN PUBLISHERS, INC.
New York, London

Published by Neal-Schuman Publishers, Inc.
100 Varick Street
New York, NY 10013

Printed and bound in the United States of America

Computer graphics by The Print Shop® Broderbund Software, Inc. 1986 and
Clickart® T/Maker Company, 1990.

Library of Congress Cataloging-in-Publication Data

Roach, Catharyn.
    Teaching library skills in grades K through 6 : a how-to-do-it
manual for school and public librarians / Catharyn Roach, JoAnne
Moore.
       p. cm. — (How-to-do-it manuals for school and public
librarians : no. 10)
    Includes bibliographical references and index.
    ISBN 1-55570-126-4
    1. Elementary school libraries--United States--Activity programs.
2. Library orientation for school children--United States.
1. Public libraries--United States--Activity programs. I. Moore,
Joanne. II. Title. III. Series.
Z675.S3R63   1993
025.5′678222—dc20   93-7768
                                           CIP

Special thanks to my family who think I can achieve anything, to my husband who helps me achieve everything, and to the faculty, staff and students at Dan D. Rogers Elementary School who are a part of my every achievement.

CR

Dedicated to those who love children and books and a profession that brings them together.

JM

CONTENTS

PREFACE

As the nation focuses on the importance of education and both the direct and indirect influence it has on the resolution of the major societal problems of crime, poverty, unemployment, teen pregnancy, at-risk students, and drop-outs, educators realize that paradigms of change must become reality. School library media specialists play a key role in moving others toward educational excellence. Change requires us to move from what was and is to what can and will be.

The year 2000 is approaching and library media specialists are on a rapid course of change as they manage emerging technology, media, and books in their library media centers and in networks that link them to other libraries and educational databases. They are managers of information access and retrieval. Students will become motivated learners when skills are taught through information that is interesting and well-written. No one can expect students to be interested in a lesson on the Dewey Decimal System, regardless of how important that knowledge is in locating the information they are seeking. They will, however, eagerly seek out topics that interest them like sports and hobbies, dinosaurs, animals, or unexplained phenomena. Masterly teaching relates the learning to the learner's background. Teaching considers where the learners are and takes them further.

Performance-based curriculum requires students to go beyond knowing and understanding to thinking, decision-making, and doing. The outcome-driven goals and objectives move teachers away from textbook-bound curriculum to resource-based instruction. The library media specialist and the teachers can become the driving forces in school improvement in academic excellence.

Literature-based learning uses a thematic approach to reach important objectives. Interdisciplinary instruction connects all disciplines. Teaching will have a greater impact on learning when students can plug into a common theme and when linkages are made. Learning doesn't occur in a vacuum. Library media becomes the major conduit for connections.

Fully integrated library media instruction involves the teacher and the library media specialist in the planning, implementation, and evaluation of the learning experiences. A critical component of significant changes in how teachers teach, students learn, and library media specialists consult and teach is administrative leadership. Principals will buy into the importance of the library media specialist role when they see demonstrated evidence of student achievement. Information and technology cannot cure what is wrong with education, but what library media specialists, teachers, parents, and administrators do with that information and technology can and will make a difference in student growth and continual improvement.

As the director of library media services in the seventh largest school district in the nation, I accept the powerful reality of addressing the needs of all learners. It is clear that library media instruction must change. The literature is full of information that points us in new directions. Creativity is a vital ingredient in using our great storehouse of literary works. Teaching is a science requiring library media specialists to use a structured approach in guiding students toward higher levels of learning, thinking, and writing. As information specialists and lovers of literature, library media specialists use their knowledge of curriculum and learning strategies to design effective learning experiences. Because library media specialists are manufacturers of ideas and because their time for creative planning is limited, the products of their imaginations should be shared. The 50 lessons in this book include instruction in the areas of library media center orientation, circulation, literature appreciation, and information skills for students in kindergarten through grade six. These lessons are not the work of a single talented mind, but of many. Library media specialists across the country were invited to contribute ideas for library media instructional plans. In this sense, the instructional plans included in this book are original interpretations of familiar lessons that have been changed to reflect the interests of today's students.

JoAnne Moore

ACKNOWLEDGMENTS

We gratefully recognize the outstanding achievement of the elementary library media specialists of the Dallas Independent School District who worked as a team to update the LMC Learner Standards and to create Instructional Planning Forms for each grade level. Special thanks must also be given to the following library media specialists who generously shared their lessons:

CONTRIBUTORS
Cathy Anderson. Ringgold, Georgia
Wildenia Bain. Dallas, Texas
Janet Clancy. Groton, Connecticut
Cynthia Daniels. Dallas, Texas
Diana Furr. University Park, Texas
Sherry Girard. Anchorage, Alaska
Merry Graves. Dallas, Texas
Lynn Hallquist. Anchorage, Alaska
Laquita Henderson. Warner Roberts, Georgia
Susan Horlock. Dallas, Texas
Sylvia Hoskins. Dumfries, Virginia
Bridgett Howard. Perry, Georgia
MaryJo George. Dallas, Texas
Veda Kull. Dallas, Texas
Jennifer Laba. Dallas, Texas
Faye Lastinger. Warner Roberts, Georgia
William Marantas. North Tonawanda, New York
Kathy Pomara. Dallas, Texas
Sherry Ryals. Dallas, Texas
Betty Ann Russ. Groton, Connecticut
Kathleen Salas. Lexington, Kentucky
Margaret Sorrells. Dallas, Texas
Linda Thompson. Perry, Georgia
Linda York. Arlington, Texas

INTRODUCTION

In this day and age of computer games and home videos, the library media specialist and the classroom teacher are constantly seeking new ways to motivate their students and to excite them about learning. The lessons in *Teaching Library Skills in Grades K through 6* are designed to do just that. The activities in these instructional plans offer a variety of learning experiences including cooperative learning and hands-on activities. Each plan is contained on a single page and many are followed by additional materials such as illustrations, charts, or patterns to use with the lesson. Ideally, the library media specialist or teacher will be able to photocopy the instructional plans, date them, make necessary notes and individual adjustments, add subject areas for classroom curriculum correlation and insert the plans in a lesson plan binder for use.

The lessons are grouped according to three of the broad areas of skills being taught—Orientation and Circulation, Literature Appreciation, and Information Skills. Within each area the lessons are arranged by grade level. Each lesson was placed in a particular grade level because it has been successfully used at that level and because it correlates well with the subject area curriculum often taught in that grade. For instance, the lesson about an attempt on the life of Abraham Lincoln works well in the fifth grade because the fifth grade social studies curriculum often includes American history and geography. A lesson on Pocahontas, however, would be appropriate for fifth grade for the same reason, but could be used in the sixth grade as well because the Native American princess spent the last days of her life living in England and is buried there. Sixth grade students often study countries of the world and a lesson on life in England at the time of Pocahontas would offer a different perspective for an introduction to England and English history. The lessons can, of course, be easily adapted to different grade levels to adjust them to individual curriculum differences, as well as degrees of difficulty. The teacher or library media specialist may want to use only parts of a lesson or may need to enhance a lesson in order to meet the particular needs and abilities of the students. Remember, also, that an introductory lesson for one grade level can be used for review for the next one and that many lessons must be repeated each year to orient new students and reacquaint returning students with the library media center arrangement and procedures. The grade level designation is only a guideline and should in no way limit the imagination or creativity of the student, teacher, or library media specialist in the pursuit of excitement in the library media center!

Most of the lessons are designed to last about 30 minutes, unless otherwise noted on the individual plans, but the library media specialist will need to adjust the time according to the skills of the students. Most of the lessons can be presented in two separate class sessions, if necessary, and many of them can be modified in content to fit time allotments from 20 to 45 minutes. Additional time will be necessary for book circulation or other scheduled activities.

Appropriate LMC learner standards have been circled for each lesson. Most skills taught in the library media center will correlate with language arts in the classroom, but if a lesson correlates with other subject areas, a note has been added beneath the *Curriculum Correlation* portion of the lesson plan.

All materials, including those for completing the extension project, have been listed. In the *Focus* area of the plan, the objective of the lesson has been written as a statement explaining the purpose of the lesson to the students. This statement is printed in bold, italicized letters.

Each lesson lists questions to ask the students as well as possible or appropriate student responses. In any lesson, it is necessary to build the students' vocabulary and background knowledge of the material being presented. There are many interesting methods of presenting vocabulary that go beyond writing the words on the chalkboard and defining them for the students. For instance, if the library media specialist is introducing the book *The Talking Eggs* to a class, he or she can select the ten words that will be unfamiliar to the students, write the words on slips of paper and put each slip in a plastic egg. Students can select the eggs one at a time and the meaning of each word can be discussed and determined by the students. Vocabulary words for a lesson about Valentine's Day could be written on heart-shaped cards and distributed as Valentine greetings to the students.

Each lesson includes an extension activity. Usually this is an optional activity which will require extra time but, in some lessons, the extension activity is the motivational part and the LMS may want to use most of the scheduled time completing this part of the lesson.

Where necessary, helpful notes have been included at the end of each lesson. However, this section of the plan is intended for the library media specialist to make his or her own comments when using the instructional plan form.

These lessons have been successful for the many library media specialists who submitted them for inclusion in this book. Of course, the library media specialist or teacher who knows the particular abilities and needs of his or her audience will certainly want to personalize the presentations in each of the lessons.

Catharyn Roach

1 THE SCHOOL LIBRARY MEDIA PROGRAM

The school library media program in modern educational settings is designed to offer a variety of services to teachers, to students, to administrators and, in somewhat more limited capacities, to the community of which it is a part. Flexibility and individualization within school library media programs are necessary and encouraged, yet there should be well-defined and pre-determined services that are available consistently in all library media centers (LMCs). Student instruction in the LMC is an integral part of the curriculum of the campus and the district and occurs both in group settings and on an individual basis. The LMC schedule must be flexible enough to allow simultaneous use of the resources by groups and individuals. Instruction with minimal use of worksheets and didactic skill should be activity-based and student-centered. Because students benefit more from library media instruction that is directly related to classroom assignments, the library media specialist (LMS) must work closely with classroom teachers to correlate the library media standards with the learner standards for each content area. As a resource specialist, the library media specialist must ultimately be involved in curriculum design as well as implementation. Resource-based instruction is quickly replacing textbook-based teaching, thus creating a vital role for the LMC in the school-wide program.

Instruction in the LMC represents practical reinforcement of library media skills and should not be taught in isolation. The LMS should plan closely with the classroom teacher to maximize the presentation of the skills. Depending on individual needs, the LMS may need to modify the instruction for the various grade levels as these standards are only basic guidelines. Instruction in library media skills falls into the following categories:

- Orientation to policies and procedures and circulation of materials
- Literature enrichment and appreciation
- Information skills in use of resources

• Use of audiovisual equipment and computer technology.

In addition to programs and services that occur on a regular basis, many special events take place in the LMC. Reading incentive programs are often coordinated by the LMS for the entire school and special school-wide events related to the library media program usually take place during Children's Book Week, National Library Week, and School Library Media Month. Communication of these events is very important. Research indicates that communication and inservice programs are strong indicators of teachers' and principals' knowledge of and attitude toward the school library media program. The LMS may use newsletters, displays, and bulletin boards to advertise LMC activities and should be an active participant in school committees and grade level or departmental planning meetings. Communication and public relations must also take place beyond the individual school through cooperation with the public library and other community agencies, as well as with parents and community members.

The services of the library media program are essential to an effective school-wide program. The library media specialist must assume a dynamic role as part of the campus instructional team to ensure that the library media program becomes an integral part of the campus curriculum.

USING LESSON PLAN TEMPLATES

Planning strategies and preparing materials for instruction in information skills are the most important aspects of a successful lesson in the library media center. Unfortunately, with the time-consuming clerical duties that are still performed by library media specialists in today's elementary schools and with scheduled classes of students, there is usually not much time left in the hectic day for writing out detailed lesson plans. The advantage of using a lesson plan form is that the outline of the plan is already written and the lessons will be consistent from week to week.

The instructional planning forms that follow were developed by a committee of experienced library media specialists in a large urban school district. They evolved from a need for current guidelines that reflect the abilities of today's students and the many resources available to them.

The lesson plan form included here consists of several elements, or parts, each with a distinct and necessary purpose:

TITLE OF LESSON

Often the LMS has a name or title of a particular lesson that will quickly identify its purpose. A space has been left on the form directly above the LMC LEARNER STANDARDS for this use.

LMC LEARNER STANDARDS

The learner standards were developed after studying those of several districts and were examined and revised many times to insure continuity and content, although there will be some variation among schools and library media centers. Because most lessons in the library media center include more than one learner standard and because some learner standards are included every week, all of the learner standards for a particular grade level are listed on the planning form. The LMS can indicate those to be included by circling, checking, or highlighting the appropriate standard or standards for the lesson.

CURRICULUM CORRELATION

The current theories of education , which include literature-based teaching and interdisciplinary teaching, offer a golden opportunity for the library media specialist to ensure that the library media program is an integral part of the total education program in the school. These are not new theories, especially to library media specialists who have been using children's books as springboards to exciting learning experiences for years and who have consistently worked with teachers to correlate the lessons presented in the library media center with those taught in the classroom. This latest twist on an old theory is that correlation is not only desirable, it is essential. The LMS can take these planning forms to the grade level meetings and identify the classroom curriculum correlation and write it on the form as the teachers are doing their weekly planning.

MATERIALS

Although the materials needed for presenting a lesson may be the last thing the library media specialist will list as the planning for a lesson is completed, that list will be the first thing needed when the preparation for the lesson begins. Materials may include any or all of the following items:

- Books needed for the lesson
- Audiovisual materials and equipment to be used
- Charts, posters, signs, flash cards, bulletin boards, and other visuals needed
- Pencils, pens, markers, chalk, etc. that the LMS or the students will use
- Props, puppets, models, or other realia used for motivation.

A large space has been allowed on the planning form for listing materials. It doesn't necessarily follow that the more *things* used in the presentation, the better the lesson will be, but in the high tech world of today's students, visuals and realia do attract their attention. Try to list *everything* needed for the lesson, even the items you usually have on hand anyway.

The next three elements of the lesson plan, *Focus, Activity,* and *Closure* are actually parts of the lesson cycle. Lesson plans are meant for use by teachers, or in this case, by library media specialists. They are not to be used as evidence of teaching, but as a guide for presenting the lesson. Many different techniques are used in organizing this information. Some library media specialists use a paragraph form; many use a step-by-step outline; and still others have their own form of shorthand. Remember, one advantage of using a form for recording information, is that the form itself is concise. Try to keep the contents just as concise.

FOCUS

To begin the lesson, the library media specialist must get the attention of the students and prepare them for the lesson by providing background through introduction of vocabulary and presentation of facts or knowledge that the students may not have, but which are essential to the lesson. The students should be made aware of the purpose of the lesson as well. In this section, the LMS may want to state the objectives of the lesson. This portion of the lesson cycle also provides transition from previous lessons to the current lesson.

ACTIVITY

This is the actual lesson, where the concept will be taught. Usually class time is limited in the library media center and careful planning and preparation will prove beneficial when the lesson is finally presented and the activities are actually taking place. The library media specialist has many responsibilities in teaching the lesson:

1. **Provide Instruction**
   - Explain the concept
   - State definitions
   - Identify critical attributes
   - Provide examples
2. **Check for Understanding**
   - Pose key questions
   - Have students explain the concepts in their own words
   - Have students discriminate between examples and non-examples
   - Encourage students to present their own examples
   - Use active participation devices
3. **Offer Guided Practice**
   - Initiate practice activities under supervision
   - Elicit responses that demonstrate understanding of the objective
   - Provide close monitoring
   - Continue to check for understanding

CLOSURE

All too soon the library media specialist must bring the lesson to a close by *pulling it all together so that those little glimmers of understanding appear in the eyes of the students.* Very quickly, the library media specialist must make a final assessment of how those objectives stated at the beginning of the lesson have been met. If there is time, the students may perform independently. Sometimes, the *closure* of the lesson overlaps with the *extension* area.

EXTENSION

The final part of the actual lesson may include some independent or group practice so students may apply the knowledge that they have learned. It may be a time when the library media specialist can test for results. Or, it may be time for some entertaining enrichment activities. In this part of the lesson, the LMS should provide an activity that will make this a *lasting lesson*.

NOTES

Just as students need feedback for their efforts, the library media specialist should evaluate the success of the lesson. It is time to analyze what worked and what didn't work and what needs improvement. The LMS may make a note of items or activities to add or to delete. The lesson may have sparked an idea for another lesson and the LMS may make note of that idea. Sometimes the lesson is just right and no other note is needed except for that tiny *smiley face*!

| Kindergarten | LIBRARY MEDIA INSTRUCTIONAL PLAN | DATE_____ |

MATERIALS:

LMC LEARNER STANDARDS

Orientation & Circulation
1. LMC Areas: INTRODUCE **Circulation Area; Fiction/Easy Section(s); Periodical Section**
2. Vocabulary: INTRODUCE **LMC; media; author; illustrator; title; fiction**
3. INTRODUCE LMC Rules
4. INTRODUCE Local Circulation Procedures
5. INTRODUCE Book Care Rules

Literature Appreciation
1. Fiction
   01. Types: Picture Books
   02. Elements: Plot (sequence)
2. Nonfiction
   01. Folklore (Fairy Tales; Folktales; Holidays; Nursery Rhymes)
   02. Poetry
3. Multicultural Literature
4. Authors/Illustrators
5. Award Books (Caldecott)

Information Skills
1. Parts of a Book: INTRODUCE **front cover; back cover; title; spine**
2. Research: INTRODUCE Comprehension Skills; Sequencing Skills; Recalling Details; Identifying Main Idea; Alphabetical Order

Technology
1. INTRODUCE Proper Use & Care of Appropriate AV Equipment
2. INTRODUCE Viewing & Listening Skills

FOCUS:

ACTIVITY:

CURRICULUM CORRELATION

_____
_____
_____
_____
_____
_____
_____
_____

CLOSURE:

EXTENSION:

NOTES:

GRADE 1	LIBRARY MEDIA INSTRUCTIONAL PLAN	DATE_____

MATERIALS:

LMC LEARNER STANDARDS

Orientation & Circulation
1. LMC Areas: REVIEW **Circulation Area; Fiction/Easy Section(s); Periodical Section**
2. Vocabulary: REVIEW **LMC; media; author; illustrator; title; fiction;** INTRODUCE **spine label; dictionary**
3. REVIEW LMC Rules
4. REVIEW Local Circulation Procedures/ Check Out Books
5. REVIEW Book Care Rules

Literature Appreciation
1. Fiction
   01. Types: Picture Books
   02. Elements: Plot; Character
2. Nonfiction
   01. Folklore (Fairy Tales; Folktales; Holidays; Nursery Rhymes)
   02. Poetry
3. Multicultural Literature
4. Authors/Illustrators
5. Award Books (Caldecott)

Information Skills
1. Location of Materials: INTRODUCE Location of Fiction Books on Shelves by Spine Label
2. Parts of a Book: REVIEW **front cover; back cover; spine; title;** INTRODUCE **title page**
3. Research: REVIEW Comprehension Skills; Sequencing Skills; Recalling Details; Identifying Main Idea; Alphabetical Order; INTRODUCE Identifying Fantasy; Picture Dictionary

Technology
1. REVIEW/INTRODUCE Proper Use & Care of Appropriate AV Equipment
2. REVIEW/INTRODUCE Viewing & Listening Skills

FOCUS:

ACTIVITY:

CURRICULUM CORRELATION

_____

_____

_____

_____

_____

_____

CLOSURE:

EXTENSION:

NOTES:

| GRADE 2 | LIBRARY MEDIA INSTRUCTIONAL PLAN | DATE_____ |

MATERIALS:

LMC LEARNER STANDARDS

Orientation & Circulation
1. LMC Areas: REVIEW **Circulation Area; Fiction/Easy Section(s); Periodical Section; INTRODUCE Reference Section; Nonfiction Section; Biography Section; Card/Computer Catalog**
2. Vocabulary: REVIEW **LMC; media; author; illustrator; title; fiction; spine label; dictionary; INTRODUCE biography; nonfiction; fable; fairy tale; table of contents; reference; chapter; card/computer catalog**
3. REVIEW LMC Rules
4. REVIEW Local Circulation Procedures/Check Out Books
5. REVIEW Book Care Rules

Literature Appreciation
1. Fiction
   01. Types: Realistic; Mystery & Fantasy
   02. Elements: Plot; Character; Setting
2. Nonfiction
   01. Folklore (Fairy Tales & Fables)
   02. Poetry
   03. Biography
   04. Informational
3. Multicultural Literature
4. Award Books (Caldecott)
5. Authors & Illustrators

Information Skills
1. Location of Materials: REVIEW Arrangement of Fiction Books; INTRODUCE Arrangement of Nonfiction Books & Arrangement of Biography Books
2. Parts of a Book: REVIEW **front cover; back cover; spine; title; title page;** INTRODUCE **table of contents**
3. Research: REVIEW Use of Dictionary; Alphabetical Order; INTRODUCE Use of Maps & Globes; Use of Tables & Graphs; Differences between Books and Periodicals; Differences Between Fact & Fiction

Technology
1. REVIEW/INTRODUCE Proper Use & Care of Appropriate AV Equipment
2. REVIEW/INTRODUCE Viewing & Listening Skills

CURRICULUM CORRELATION

_____

_____

_____

_____

_____

_____

FOCUS:

ACTIVITY:

CLOSURE:

EXTENSION:

NOTES:

GRADE 3	LIBRARY MEDIA INSTRUCTIONAL PLAN	DATE_____

MATERIALS:

LMC LEARNER STANDARDS

Orientation & Circulation
1. LMC Areas: REVIEW **Circulation Area; Fiction/Easy Section(s); Periodical Section; Reference Section; Card/Computer Catalog; Nonfiction Section; Biography Section**
2. Vocabulary: REVIEW **media; reference; fiction; nonfiction; periodicals; chapter;** INTRODUCE **publisher; call number; almanac; copyright date; atlas**
3. REVIEW LMC Rules
4. REVIEW Local Circulation Procedures/ Check Out Books
5. REVIEW Book Care Rules

Literature Appreciation
1. Fiction
   01. Types: Mystery; Realistic
   02. Elements: Plot; Character & Setting
2. Nonfiction
   01. Folklore (Fables, Folktales, Fairy Tales)
   02. Poetry
   03. Biography
   04. Informational
3. Multicultural Literature
4. Authors/Illustrators
5. Award Books (Caldecott, Greenaway)

Information Skills
1. Location of Materials: REVIEW/EXTEND Arrangement of Fiction Books; Arrangement of Nonfiction Books & Arrangement of Biography Books
2. Parts of a Book: REVIEW **table of contents, title page;** INTRODUCE **glossary; index**
3. Research: REVIEW /EXTEND Use of Dictionary; Alphabetical Order; INTRODUCE Use of Encyclopedia; Use of Periodicals; Use of Special Reference Books; Use of Atlas
4. Card/Computer Catalog: INTRODUCE Types of Cards/Searches & Card/Record Information

Technology
1. REVIEW /INTRODUCE Proper Use & Care of Appropriate AV Equipment
2. REVIEW /INTRODUCE Viewing & Listening Skills

CURRICULUM CORRELATION

_____

_____

_____

_____

_____

FOCUS:

ACTIVITY:

CLOSURE:

EXTENSION:

NOTES:

GRADE 4	LIBRARY MEDIA INSTRUCTIONAL PLAN	DATE_____

MATERIALS:

LMC LEARNER STANDARDS

Orientation & Circulation
1. LMC Areas: REVIEW **Circulation Area; Fiction/Easy Section(s); Periodical Section; Reference Section; Nonfiction Section; Biography Section; Card/Computer Catalog**
2. Vocabulary: REVIEW **media; reference; fiction; nonfiction; periodicals; publisher; biography; atlas; almanac; call number; copyright date;** INTRODUCE **unabridged dictionary; thesaurus; verso**
3. REVIEW LMC Rules
4. REVIEW Local Circulation Procedures/Check Out Books
5. REVIEW Book Care Rules

Literature Appreciation
1. Fiction
   01. Types: Historical, Realistic; Humorous; Adventure
   02. Elements: Character; Plot; Setting
2. Nonfiction
   01. Folklore (Fables, Folktales, Fairy Tales)
   02. Poetry
   03. Biography
   04. Informational
3. Multicultural Literature
4. Authors/Illustrators
5. Award Books (Newbery; Coretta Scott King)

Information Skills
1. Location of Materials: REVIEW/EXTEND Arrangement of Fiction Books; Arrangement of Nonfiction Books & Arrangement of Biography Books; INTRODUCE Arrangement of Audiovisual Materials
2. Parts of a Book: REVIEW **table of contents; title page; glossary, index;** INTRODUCE **dedication**
3. Research: REVIEW/EXTEND Alphabetical Order; Use of the Encyclopedia; Use of the Dictionary; Use of Periodicals; Use of Special Reference Books ; INTRODUCE Use of Atlas; Use of Almanac; Children's Magazine Guide
4. Card/Computer Catalog: REVIEW /EXTEND Types of Cards/Searches & Card/Record Information

Technology
1. REVIEW/INTRODUCE Proper Use & Care of Appropriate AV Equipment & Software
2. REVIEW/INTRODUCE Viewing & Listening Skills

CURRICULUM CORRELATION

_____
_____
_____
_____
_____

FOCUS:

ACTIVITY:

CLOSURE:

EXTENSION:

NOTES:

GRADE 5	LIBRARY MEDIA INSTRUCTIONAL PLAN	DATE_____

MATERIALS:

LMC LEARNER STANDARDS

Orientation & Circulation
1. LMC Areas: REVIEW **Circulation Area; Fiction/Easy Section(s); Periodical Section; Nonfiction Section; Biography Section Reference Section; Card/Computer Catalog**
2. Vocabulary: REVIEW **media; reference; fiction; nonfiction; periodicals; publisher; biography; atlas; almanac;** INTRODUCE **audio; visual; classics**
3. REVIEW LMC Rules
4. REVIEW Local Circulation Procedures/ Check Out Books
5. REVIEW Book Care Rules

FOCUS:

Literature Appreciation
1. Fiction
   01. Types: Science Fiction; Historical; Realistic
   02. Character; Plot; Setting; Theme
2. Nonfiction
   01. Folklore (Fables, Folktales, Fairy Tales; Tall Tales)
   02. Poetry
   03. Biography
   04. Informational
3. Multicultural Literature
4. Award Books (Newbery; Wilder)
5. Authors/Illustrators

ACTIVITY:

Information Skills
1. Location of Materials: REVIEW/EXTEND Arrangement of Fiction Books; Arrangement of Nonfiction Books; Arrangement of Biography Books; Arrangement of AV Materials
2. Parts of a Book: INTRODUCE **preface & copyright page**
3. Research: REVIEW /EXTEND Use of Encyclopedia; Use of Dictionary; Use of Periodicals; Use of Special Reference Books; Use of Atlas; Use of Almanac; Children's Magazine Guide; INTRODUCE Use of Thesaurus
4. Card/Computer Catalog: REVIEW/EXTEND Types of Cards/Searches & Card/Record Information
5. Dewey Decimal System: INTRODUCE Ten Classes

CLOSURE:

Technology
1. REVIEW/INTRODUCE Proper Use & Care of Appropriate AV Equipment
2. REVIEW/INTRODUCE Viewing & Listening Skills

EXTENSION:

CURRICULUM CORRELATION

_____

_____

_____

_____

_____

NOTES:

| GRADE 6 | LIBRARY MEDIA INSTRUCTIONAL PLAN | DATE_____ |

MATERIALS:

LMC LEARNER STANDARDS
Orientation & Circulation
1. LMC Areas: REVIEW **Circulation Area; Fiction/Easy Section(s); Periodical Section; Reference Section; Nonfiction Section; Biography Section; Card/Computer Catalog**
2. Vocabulary REVIEW **media; fiction; reference; nonfiction; periodicals; publisher; biography; atlas; audio; visual; classics;** INTRODUCE **autobiography**
3. REVIEW LMC Rules
4. REVIEW Local Circulation Procedures/ Check Out Books
5. REVIEW Book Care Rules

FOCUS:

Literature Appreciation
1. Fiction
   01. All Types
   02. Character; Plot; Setting; Theme; Style
2. Nonfiction
   01. Folklore (Fables, Folktales, Fairy Tales; Tall Tales; Mythology & Legends)
   02. Poetry
   03. Biography/Autobiography
3. Multicultural Literature
4. Award Books (Newbery; Carnegie; Coretta Scott King)
5. Authors/Illustrators

ACTIVITY:

Information Skills
1. Location of Materials: REVIEW/EXTEND Arrangement of Fiction Books; Arrangement of Nonfiction Books; Arrangement of Biography Books & Arrangement of AV Materials
2. Parts of a Book: REVIEW **preface; copyright page;** INTRODUCE **bibliography; footnotes; preface; appendices**
3. Research: REVIEW/EXTEND Use of Encyclopedia; Use of Periodicals; Use of Special Reference Books; Use of Atlas; Use of Almanac; Use of Thesaurus; Children's Magazine Guide; REINFORCE Outlining for Research
4. Card/Computer Catalog: REVIEW/EXTEND Types of Cards/Searches & Card/Record Information
5. Dewey Decimal System: REVIEW/EXTEND Ten Classes & Recognize Subject of Each

CLOSURE:

Technology
1. REVIEW/INTRODUCE Proper Use & Care of Appropriate AV Equipment
2. REVIEW/INTRODUCE Viewing & Listening Skills

EXTENSION:

CURRICULUM CORRELATION
_____
_____
_____
_____
_____

NOTES:

2 ORIENTATION AND CIRCULATION

In secondary schools, the orientation process usually takes place at the beginning of the school year when each class is rotated into the library media center and introduced to the various resources and services available. In the elementary school, however, where students traditionally visit the library media center on a regular basis, orientation may take place throughout the year. The rules of behavior should be displayed in a prominent location in the LMC. Although they are usually introduced at the beginning of the year, these rules must be periodically reinforced during the school year, as the students appear to "forget" them. The library media specialist is constantly pointing out the arrangement and location of the LMC and the kinds of resources available in each area. Each area should be clearly labelled.

To ensure basic communication between the library media specialist and the students, essential vocabulary must be reviewed almost weekly. It's a good idea to have a special location in the LMC where vocabulary words are displayed all the time. A long, narrow bulletin board, a closed door, or even the end of a bookshelf can be a perfect Vocabulary Board. Words can be printed on colorful paper, laminated and added to the board as they are introduced to the students. Once the words are displayed on the Vocabulary Board, the LMS can refer to them anytime. An alternative use of the Vocabulary Board involves highlighting a particular word and its definition. The vocabulary word can be changed about every two weeks.

In most elementary school library media centers, circulation of books and other materials is a part of the students' weekly visit and probably occurs on an individual basis as well. Specific circulation procedures vary from school to school, but the basic process is the same, whether book cards with circulation files or computers are used. The process is usually explained at the beginning of the school year, but must be reviewed informally almost every week. Once the students have borrowed books, they are responsible for their care. The prices of books, especially picture books, has *skyrocketed* in recent years and books are out-of-print within a short time. Proper book care cannot be over-emphasized with the students.

Seven lessons that deal with the areas of orientation to the LMC and with book care and circulation have been included in this chapter. Each lesson has been designated for a specific grade, but can be adapted for use with almost any level.

A bibliography of the various works used in these lessons is included at the end of the chapter. Of course, other appropriate titles may be substituted based on individual collections.

Kindergarten: *The Book Doctor.* Using a doctor's bag and smock, the library media specialist demonstrates proper book care. Students are encouraged to report any damage to the library media specialist so proper repairs can be made.

First Grade: *Clowning Around.* Students are taught that proper behavior in the library media center does not include *acting like a clown.* This lesson is part of a behavior management system for primary students.

Second Grade: *Happy Book/Sad Book.* Students discuss that proper book care makes books *happy* and that neglect and abuse makes books *sad.* Students are able to look at books which have not been taken care of.

Third Grade: *Pamper Your Books.* Proper book care is stressed and students review the ways that they can take extra special care of their library books so that others will also be able to enjoy them.

Fourth Grade: *Floor Plan Follies.* Using a *map* of the library media center, students identify its various parts and the kinds of materials located in each area. This activity is great for reacquainting students with the library media center after summer break.

Fifth Grade: *Media Coverage.* The term *media* is reviewed with the students and they have a chance to identify the various types of materials available in the Library Media Center.

Sixth Grade: *Circle of Books.* A visual description of book circulation is presented and the students outline the steps in the procedure for checking out books based on their working knowledge of the steps involved. Great for reorientation after summer break.

| **Kindergarten** | **LIBRARY MEDIA INSTRUCTIONAL PLAN** | **DATE**_____ |

The Book Doctor

LMC LEARNER STANDARDS

Orientation & Circulation
1. LMC Areas: INTRODUCE **Circulation Area; Fiction/Easy Section(s); Periodical Section**
2. Vocabulary: INTRODUCE **LMC; media; author; illustrator; title; fiction**
3. INTRODUCE LMC Rules
4. INTRODUCE Local Circulation Procedures
5. INTRODUCE Book Care Rules

Literature Appreciation
1. Fiction
   01. Types: Picture Books
   02. Elements: Plot (sequence)
2. Nonfiction
   01. Folklore (Fairy Tales; Folktales; Holidays; Nursery Rhymes)
   02. Poetry
3. Multicultural Literature
4. Authors/Illustrators
5. Award Books (Caldecott)

Information Skills
1. Parts of a Book: INTRODUCE **front cover; back cover; title; spine**
2. Research: INTRODUCE Comprehension Skills; Sequencing Skills; Recalling Details; Identifying Main Idea; Alphabetical Order

Technology
1. INTRODUCE Proper Use & Care of Appropriate AV Equipment
2. INTRODUCE Viewing & Listening Skills

CURRICULUM CORRELATION

_____

_____

_____

_____

_____

_____

_____

_____

MATERIALS:
Book, Benjamin's Book by Alan Baker
Doctor's Smock and Stethoscope
Doctor's Bag (if available) filled with book repair items, such as transparent tape, cloth tape, glue, cleaner, mending sticks, binder tape, paper hinge tape, brushes, scissors, repair wings, etc.
Damaged Book - Find a damaged book that has been withdrawn from the collection and is beyond repair, preferably one that has been water-damaged. Tear the corners of some of the pages and turn down some corners. Mark in the book with crayon and write in it with pencil. Wrinkle some of the pages and cut out some of the pictures. Smear grease on a page and pull the pages away from the binding. NOW you have a *damaged* book!
Extension Project: Rx For Healthy Books Bookmarks (see next page)

FOCUS:
Ask the students what happens when they get hurt. Sometimes their moms or dads can fix them up with band aids, but if they're really hurt, they might have to go to a doctor. Have the students think of ways a book could be *hurt*. *Tell the students that you're the book doctor and today we're going to talk about taking care of books so that they don't get hurt.*

ACTIVITY:
Introduce Benjamin as a hamster who loved books. One day Benjamin had an accident with his book and he tried to fix it himself. Read the book to see what a mess he made.

Afterwards, discuss what Benjamin should have done when he got his book dirty. He should not have tried to fix it himself, he should have taken it to the Book Doctor to be cleaned.

Tell the students that sometimes when books get dirty or torn, they can be repaired, but they should not try to fix the books themselves because it takes special tools and equipment. Tell the students that you're the book doctor and you can fix many books which are damaged. Tell them to always bring books to you when they need to be repaired. Show them the Doctor's bag and all the tools necessary for this job.

CLOSURE:
Tell the students that you cannot always repair the books and sometimes they are so damaged that they must be thrown away. Show them the damaged book. Point out the damage that can be repaired, such as pencil marks and tears, and the damage that cannot be repaired, such as water damage and missing pages or pictures.

Explain that repairing books takes a lot of time and while the book is being repaired, no one can borrow it from the LMC or read it. Tell the students that often, if the spine or backbone of the book is broken, you must send it to a bindery where it can be repaired. This not only takes several months, but it costs extra money.

EXTENSION:
Remind the students that when they are hurt and go to the doctor's office, sometimes after the doctor gives them medicine to make them well, he/she can tell them ways to stay healthy and not get sick or hurt again. Go through the damaged book again and have the students think about ways that the damage could have been avoided if the students who read the book had been more careful. Distribute the bookmarks.

NOTES:

R_x

Prescription for Healthy Books

Wash your hands before reading your book.
Never color or mark in your book.
Never tear the pages of your book.
Protect your book from the rain and sun.
Protect your book from babies and pets.
Never lick your fingers to turn the pages of a book.
Turn the pages from the top right corner.
Don't read your book while you're eating or drinking.
Always use a bookmark to keep your place.

R_x

Prescription for Healthy Books

Wash your hands before reading your book.
Never color or mark in your book.
Never tear the pages of your book.
Protect your book from the rain and sun.
Protect your book from babies and pets.
Never lick your fingers to turn the pages of a book.
Turn the pages from the top right corner.
Don't read your book while you're eating or drinking.
Always use a bookmark to keep your place.

R_x

Prescription for Healthy Books

Wash your hands before reading your book.
Never color or mark in your book.
Never tear the pages of your book.
Protect your book from the rain and sun.
Protect your book from babies and pets.
Never lick your fingers to turn the pages of a book.
Turn the pages from the top right corner.
Don't read your book while you're eating or drinking.
Always use a bookmark to keep your place.

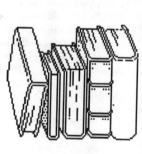

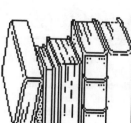

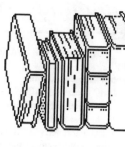

R_x

Prescription for Healthy Books

Wash your hands before reading your book.
Never color or mark in your book.
Never tear the pages of your book.
Protect your book from the rain and sun.
Protect your book from babies and pets.
Never lick your fingers to turn the pages of a book.
Turn the pages from the top right corner.
Don't read your book while you're eating or drinking.
Always use a bookmark to keep your place.

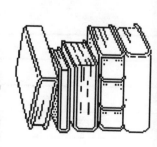

GRADE 1	LIBRARY MEDIA INSTRUCTIONAL PLAN	DATE_____

Clowning Around

LMC LEARNER STANDARDS

Orientation & Circulation
1. LMC Areas: REVIEW **Circulation Area; Fiction/Easy Section(s); Periodical Section**
2. Vocabulary: REVIEW **LMC; media; author; illustrator; title; fiction;** INTRODUCE **spine label; dictionary**
3. REVIEW LMC Rules
4. REVIEW Local Circulation Procedures/Check Out Books
5. REVIEW Book Care Rules

Literature Appreciation
1. Fiction
   01. Types: Picture Books
   02. Elements: Plot; Character
2. Nonfiction
   01. Folklore (Fairy Tales; Folktales; Holidays; Nursery Rhymes)
   02. Poetry
3. Multicultural Literature
4. Authors/Illustrators
5. Award Books (Caldecott)

Information Skills
1. Location of Materials: INTRODUCE Location of Fiction Books on Shelves by Spine Label
2. Parts of a Book: REVIEW **front cover; back cover; spine; title;** INTRODUCE **title page**
3. Research: REVIEW Comprehension Skills; Sequencing Skills; Recalling Details; Identifying Main Idea; Alphabetical Order; INTRODUCE Identifying Fantasy; Picture Dictionary

Technology
1. REVIEW/INTRODUCE Proper Use & Care of Appropriate AV Equiment
2. REVIEW/INTRODUCE Viewing & Listening Skills

CURRICULUM CORRELATION

_____
_____
_____
_____
_____
_____

MATERIALS:
Clown LMC Rules Bulletin Board (see next page)
Clown Puppet and Crayons
Book, The Clown Arounds by Joanna Cole
Extension Project: Tagboard; Markers; Small Picture Hooks

FOCUS:
Use the clown puppet to welcome the students to the LMC. Explain that he is glad to be visiting the students and that he knows he must be on his best behavior in the LMC. He cannot *clown around*. Ask students what the clown means. Discuss what clowns usually do at a circus. Ask them if this is appropriate behavior for the LMC. *Tell the students that today we'll discuss the right way to act in the Library Media Center so they'll always be able to follow the rules.*

ACTIVITY:
Have the students look at the bulletin board. Point out that the clown there is juggling five different colored balls. On each ball there is a rule of appropriate behavior in the LMC. Read and discuss each rule with the students.
> We will come into and leave the Library Media Center in a quiet straight line. (Green Ball)
> We will work quietly and cooperatively in the Library Media Center. We will not fight or play or run. (Blue Ball)
> We will talk in a whisper in the Library Media Center so we will not disturb other students. (Yellow Ball)
> We will bring our library books back to the Library Media Center on time. (Red Ball)
> We will keep the books neat and straight on the shelves so others can find them. (Orange Ball)

Using the puppet again, ask the students if they can follow all of those rules. Tell them that they will write their names on the bulletin board. Explain that signing their signature on something is like making a promise. Have the students sign their names on the board with crayons. They may sign in groups of three or four. As they are signing their names, discuss any questions that the students have.

CLOSURE:
When all the students have signed the board, read the book The Clown Arounds. Afterwards, have the students individually recall the rules and identify the color of the rule as they say it. They may get in line as they say the rules.

EXTENSION:
Prepare a *Schedule Card* (see next page) for each class. The 9"x11" card will list the teacher's name and class section. There will also be a space for the day and time that the class comes to the LMC. Place a small hook at the bottom of the card. These can be made with blank spaces for the information and laminated so they can be completed using a washable marker and then used for several years. Also make some *Clowns*. Cut 9" circles from tagboard. Draw or trace and color a picture of a clown on each circle. (Look for a coloring book of clown pictures at the book store, toy store or dime store.) Write "We don't clown around in the Library Media Center" on each *Clown*. Laminate the circles and punch a hole in the top of each one. Give the *Schedule Card* to the teacher when the class first visits the LMC and ask him/her to hang it in a prominent spot in the classroom. Explain to the students that each time they visit the LMC, they will be able to earn a *Clown* to take back to the classroom and hang on the *Schedule Card* so that every visitor to their classroom will know that the students in that class know how to behave in the LMC. The class line leader must return the *clown* at each visit to the LMC so the class can have a chance to earn a different one.

NOTES:
This activity can be done using a variety of themes:
We're Not Media Monsters (Monsters)
We're UnBEARably Good in the LMC (Bears)
We're DINOmite in the LMC (Dinosaurs)

We Don't Clown Around in the Library Media Center

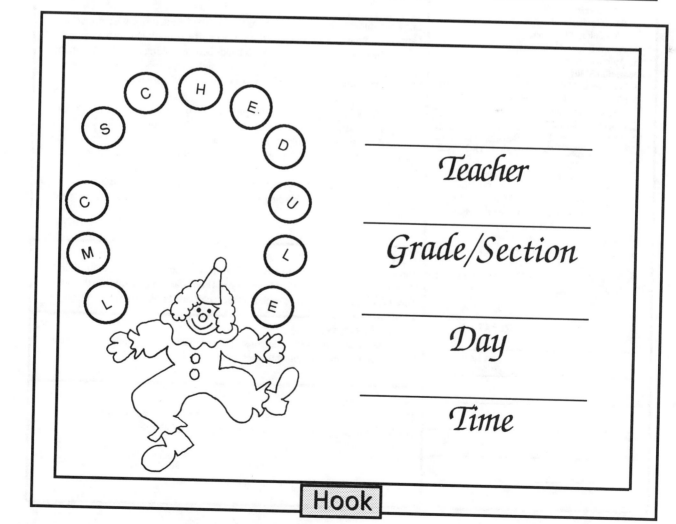

Teacher

Grade/Section

Day

Time

Hook

GRADE 2	LIBRARY MEDIA INSTRUCTIONAL PLAN	DATE_____

Happy Book / Sad Book

LMC LEARNER STANDARDS

Orientation & Circulation
1. LMC Areas: REVIEW **Circulation Area;**
   Fiction/Easy Section(s); Periodical Section;
   INTRODUCE **Reference Section; Nonfiction**
   Section; Biography Section; Card/Computer
   Catalog
2. Vocabulary: REVIEW **LMC; media;**
   author; illustrator; title; fiction; spine label;
   dictionary; INTRODUCE **biography;**
   nonfiction; fable; fairy tale; table of contents;
   reference; chapter; card/computer catalog
3. REVIEW LMC Rules
4. REVIEW Local Circulation Procedures/Check
   Out Books
5. REVIEW Book Care Rules

Literature Appreciation
1. Fiction
   01. Types: Realistic; Mystery & Fantasy
   02. Elements: Plot; Character; Setting
2. Nonfiction
   01. Folklore (Fairy Tales & Fables)
   02. Poetry
   03. Biography
   04. Informational
3. Multicultural Literature
4. Award Books (Caldecott)
5. Authors & Illustrators

Information Skills
1. Location of Materials: REVIEW Arrangement
   of Fiction Books; INTRODUCE Arrangement
   of Nonfiction Books & Arrangement of
   Biography Books
2. Parts of a Book: REVIEW front cover; back
   cover; spine; title; title page; INTRODUCE
   table of contents
3. Research: REVIEW Use of Dictionary;
   Alphabetical Order; INTRODUCE Use of
   Maps & Globes; Use of Tables & Graphs;
   Differences between Books and Periodicals;
   Differences Between Fact & Fiction

Technology
1. REVIEW/INTRODUCE Proper Use & Care of
   Appropriate AV Equipment
2. REVIEW/INTRODUCE Viewing & Listening
   Skills

CURRICULUM CORRELATION

_____

_____

_____

_____

_____

_____

MATERIALS:
HAPPY BOOK - SAD BOOK Bulletin Board (see next page)
Three Smiling Face and Seven Frowning Face Circles (see next pages)
Thumbtacks; Happy Face Stickers
Several Worn, Discarded Books and Several New, Clean Books
Chart of Book Care Rules (see next pages)
Extension Project: Drawing Paper and Crayons

FOCUS:
Show the students the clean, new books and ask how many of them like to borrow
library books like these. Have the students share things they can do to keep the
books clean and *happy*. *Tell them that we will be reviewing book care rules.*

ACTIVITY:
Draw the students' attention to the bulletin board. Most of the books pictured there
show signs of abuse, but a few of them illustrate proper book care. Tell the
students that each book on the board has a story.

Point out each book to the students and tell its story. You can use the sample
stories included, but you'll probably want to change the names.

After you tell a story about each book, ask the students to decide if the book is
happy or *sad*. Have one student thumbtack the appropriate Smiling or Frowning
Face to the picture. Continue until all the books on the bulletin board have been
identified.

Show the students the worn, dirty books and have them describe what might have
happened to damage the books. For instance, if the book has dirty pages, the
student may have forgotten to wash his hands before looking at the book. Or, the
student may have read the book while eating and spilled food on the book. Point
out damage done to the *front covers, back covers*, and *spines* of the books.

This is a great time to demonstrate the proper way to turn the pages of a book. Get
the top right corner of the page with the thumb and index finger. Slide your hand
loosely down the right side of the page and across the bottom of the page to the
center of the book. Turn the page slowly and carefully using your entire hand.

Lead the students to make statements about proper book care. For instance,
"Wash your hands before reading your book" or "Protect your books from wet
weather."

CLOSURE:
Show the students the chart of Book Care Rules and point out the similarities
between the statements they made about good book care and the rules on the chart.
Turn the chart over and have each student recall one book care rule.

EXTENSION:
The students can make posters demonstrating proper book care and the posters can
be displayed throughout the entire school.

NOTES:
The bulletin board and happy/sad faces must be prepared ahead of time.
The lesson is easily adaptable for second grade or kindergarten.

Happy Book - Sad Book

HAPPY BOOK - SAD BOOK BULLETIN BOARD	
Description	**Sample Story for Each Picture**
Picture of a book with torn pages	Jenny checked out this book. She was in such a hurry to play with her friend after school that she left her school books on the front porch and her dog Sandy pulled them out in the yard and chewed on the pages of her library book.
Picture of a book in a clear plastic bag	On the day Martin had to return his book to the library media center, it was raining. So Martin put his book in a clear plastic bag to carry it to school. When he took his book out, it was totally dry.
Picture of a book with crayon marks on the pages	Steven forgot to put his library book up when he went to watch TV and his little sister, Susan, got into his things and colored all over the pages of his library book with a crayon. It could not be erased.
Picture of a closed book with wrinkled pages	Marsha did not put her library book in her backpack after school and she dropped the book in a mud puddle on her way home. She tried to dry it out, but the pages were hopelessly wrinkled.
Picture of a closed book with a pencil sticking out the top	When Jonathan's teacher told him to put up his library book and work on his math, he stuck a pencil in between the pages and closed the book to keep his place. The pages of the book came loose and fell out.
Picture of a book laying face down	Marilyn knew not to put a pencil in her book, but when she hurried to go out and play, she turned the book she was reading face down on her desk. Later, when she picked up the book to read it, the binding was loose and pulling away from the cover.
Picture of book with bookmark	Janet didn't have a bookmark, but she got a piece of paper and cut out a large rectangle. It made a perfect bookmark because it was not too thick and fit between the pages without hurting the book.
Picture of a book with dog-eared pages	Mark didn't have a bookmark to keep his place in his library book when he had to stop and eat dinner so he turned down the corner of the page. Later, that corner tore off and some of the words from that page were missing.
Picture of an open book with smudged pages	James didn't wash his hands after eating his lunch of spaghetti. When he went back to finish reading his library book, he got greasy, sticky smudges on the pages. Later the pages stuck together and tore apart.
Picture of a clean, new book with no tears or smudges	Ms. Jones, the principal, borrowed this book and carefully put it in her bag to take home. She kept it in a safe place while she cooked dinner. Then she washed her hands, read the book and put it back in her bag to return to school the next day.

Book Care Rules

Don't eat or drink while reading a book
Never cut or tear pages from a book
Wash your hands before reading a book
Use a bookmark to keep your place
Never turn down the corner of a page
Never leave a pencil in a closed book
Never turn a book on its "face"
Never lick your fingers to turn the pages of a book
Turn the pages from the top right corner
Keep books safe from babies and pets
Protect books from the weather
Never mark or color in a book

GRADE 3	LIBRARY MEDIA INSTRUCTIONAL PLAN	DATE_____

Pamper Your Books

LMC LEARNER STANDARDS

Orientation & Circulation
1. LMC Areas: REVIEW **Circulation Area; Fiction/Easy Section(s); Periodical Section; Reference Section; Nonfiction Section; Biography Section; Card/Computer Catalog**
2. Vocabulary: REVIEW **media; reference; fiction; nonfiction; periodicals; chapter;** INTRODUCE **publisher; call number; almanac; copyright date; atlas**
3. REVIEW LMC Rules
4. REVIEW Local Circulation Procedures/ Check Out Books
5. REVIEW Book Care Rules

Literature Appreciation
1. Fiction
   01. Types: Mystery; Realistic
   02. Elements: Plot; Character & Setting
2. Nonfiction
   01. Folklore (Fables, Folktales, Fairy Tales)
   02. Poetry
   03. Biography
   04. Informational
3. Multicultural Literature
4. Authors/Illustrators
5. Award Books (Caldecott, Greenaway)

Information Skills
1. Location of Materials: REVIEW/EXTEND Arrangement of Fiction Books; Arrangement of Nonfiction Books & Arrangement of Biography Books
2. Parts of a Book: REVIEW **table of contents, title page ;** INTRODUCE **glossary; index**
3. Research: REVIEW /EXTEND Use of Dictionary Alphabetical Order; INTRODUCE Use of Encyclopedia; Use of Periodicals; Use of Special Reference Books; Use of Atlas
4. Card/Computer/Catalog: INTRODUCE Types of Cards/Searches & Card/Record Information

Technology
1. REVIEW / INTRODUCE Proper Use & Care of Appropriate AV Equipment
2. REVIEW / INTRODUCE Viewing & Listening Skills

CURRICULUM CORRELATION

_____

_____

_____

_____

_____

_____

MATERIALS:
Book, Petunia by Roger Duvoisin
Chart of Book Care Rules
Extension Project:
Drawing Paper, Pencils, Crayons, Book Jackets, Disposable Baby Diapers

FOCUS:
Ask the students how many of them like to borrow books from the Library Media Center. Ask how many of them like to read those books. Ask if they know how to take care of those books. *Tell the students that today we're going to talk about book care but first were going to hear about a goose who loved books, too.*

ACTIVITY:
Show the students the book Petunia. Introduce the character, Petunia, the silly goose who lived an a farm with her animal friends. Explain that one day Petunia found a book. She knew that books made people very smart, so she thought that suddenly she was smart because now she had a book. Ask the students if they can learn anything from a book just by holding it. (They'll know that they can't!) Ask them how they can learn something from a book. (They'll know that they have to be able to read.) Explain that because Petunia can't read, she gets herself and her friends into a big mess. Read the book.

Tell the students that, although Petunia couldn't read, she did try to take care of her book because she knew books were valuable and important. Ask the students to think of some words that mean *to take care of* (protect, guard, pamper, defend).

Tell the students that you like the idea of *pampering* your library books. Look up *pamper* in the dictionary. Discuss that *pampering* offers extra special love and attention. Have the students tell you the ways they will pamper their library books.

CLOSURE:
Show the students the chart of book care rules and discuss any that they failed to mention.

BOOK CARE RULES
Don't eat or drink while reading a book
Never cut or tear pages from a book
Wash your hands before reading a book
Use a bookmark to keep your place
Never turn down the corner of a page
Never leave a pencil in a closed book
Never turn a book on it *face*
Never lick your fingers to turn the pages of a book
Turn the pages from the top right corner
Keep books safe from babies and pets
Protect books from the weather
Never mark or color in a book

EXTENSION:
If time allows, give each student a sheet of 9" x 12" drawing paper. Assign each of them a book care rule to illustrate. Display the pictures on the bulletin board along with some book jackets placed inside some disposable baby diapers. Use the caption *Pamper Your Library Books.*

NOTES:

| GRADE 4 | LIBRARY MEDIA INSTRUCTIONAL PLAN | DATE_____ |

Floor Plan Follies

LMC LEARNER STANDARDS

Orientation & Circulation
1. LMC Areas: REVIEW **Circulation Area; Fiction/Easy Section(s); Periodical Section; Reference Section; Nonfiction Section; Biography Section; Card/Computer Catalog**
2. Vocabulary: REVIEW **media; reference; fiction; nonfiction; periodicals; publisher; biography; atlas; almanac; call number; copyright date;** INTRODUCE **unabridged dictionary; thesaurus; verso**
3. REVIEW LMC Rules
4. REVIEW Local Circulation Procedures/Check Out Books
5. REVIEW Book Care Rules

Literature Appreciation
1. Fiction
  01. Types: Historical, Realistic; Humorous; Adventure
  02. Elements: Character; Plot; Setting
2. Nonfiction
  01. Folklore (Fables, Folktales, Fairy Tales)
  02. Poetry
  03. Biography
  04. Informational
3. Multicultural Literature
4. Authors/Illustrators
5. Award Books (Newbery; Coretta Scott King)

Information Skills
1. Location of Materials: REVIEW / EXTEND Arrangement of Fiction Books; Arrangement of Nonfiction Books & Arrangement of Biography Books; INTRODUCE Arrangement of Audiovisual Materials
2. Parts of a Book: REVIEW **table of contents; title page; glossary, index;** INTRODUCE **dedication**
3. Research: REVIEW/EXTEND Alphabetical Order; Use of the Encyclopedia; Use of the Dictionary; Use of Periodicals; Use of Special Reference Books; INTRODUCE Use of Atlas; Use of Almanac; Children's Magazine Guide
4. Card/Computer Catalog: REVIEW /EXTEND Types of Cards/Searches & Card/Record Information

Technology
1. REVIEW/INTRODUCE Proper Use & Care of Appropriate AV Equipment & Software
2. REVIEW/INTRODUCE Viewing & Listening Skills

CURRICULUM CORRELATION

_____

_____

_____

_____

_____

MATERIALS:
Activity Sheets, "LMC Floor Plan" (see next page)
Answer Key for Activity Sheet
Pencils
Sample Media Spines (see next pages)

FOCUS:
Have the students look around the Library Media Center. Call out various sections of the LMC (*Reference Section; Nonfiction Books; Card/Computer Catalog*) and have the students point them out. Ask the students to imagine that King Kong has just ripped the roof off the school and is looking down in the LMC. Of course, the LMS and the students would be gone in a flash so all the big ape can see is the room and its contents. Ask the students what various objects would look like to King Kong as he is looking down on them. (The card catalog would look like a rectangle; the circulation desk would look like a semi-circle; the book shelves would look like long, thin rectangles.) *Tell the students that today we'll see how well they can find their way around the LMC by identifying the parts of the LMC on a floor plan.*

ACTIVITY:
Distribute the Activity Sheets and help the students *get their bearings* by identifying the top of the paper as the front of the LMC and the bottom as the back. Identify other key locations, such as doors and windows.

Read the areas that the students are to identify. Explain that once the students have completed the Floor Plans, they must check their answers with the Answer Key.

After the students have checked their Floor Plans, they will get a *Sample Media Spine* from you and find that book on the book shelves. Each student will insert the *spine* in it's exact location and raise a hand for verification of its correct location.

Before the students begin, remind them of the arrangement of materials on the shelves, including books and AV items. Point out the way to *read* the shelves from left to right and down to the next shelf.

Have the students complete the assignment.

CLOSURE:
Re-cap the skills and knowledge utilized in the search, including map reading, identification of types of media and arrangement of book shelves. Stress that this logic can be used to help students find information in other library media centers as well. Stress also that they can continue to use these location skills as adults when they need to use the public library.

EXTENSION:
This same activity can be done as a contest. Instead of having the students find the areas individually, complete the floor plan as a group activity. Then have the students find the location of the *Sample Media Spines*. The student with the most *verified hits* within a specified time frame is the winner. A variation of the contest would have the student copy information from the Card/Computer Catalog and then find the item with the aid of the Floor Plan.

NOTES:
Several lessons must have been completed prior to this lesson: Types of Media; Shelf Arrangement; and Call Numbers.

The Sample Media Spines must be made in advance. To have a contest, there must be several different spines available for each student.

Name _____

_____

Class _____

Dan D. Rogers Library Media Center

1. Nonfiction Section

2. Fiction Section

3. Easy Fiction Section

4. Circulation Desk

5. Circulation Charts

6. Computers

7. Newbery Books

8. New Books

9. Periodicals

10. Reference Books

11. Card Catalog

12. Professional Books

13. Bluebonnet Books

14. Vertical File

15. Biography Section

LMC Floor Plan

Directions:
Find the areas of the
LMC listed above.
Identify each area by
writing its number
in the circle in front
of its location on
the Floor Plan.

Tales of a Fourth Grade Nothing

by Judy Blume

Filmstrip

SFS
FIC
BLU

Knots on a Counting Rope

by Bill Martin, Jr.

E
MAR

DINOSAURS

by Gail Gibbons

567.9
GIB

World Book Encyclopedia

A

Vol. 1

REF
031
WOR

Thirteen Ways to Sink a Sub

by Jamie Gilson

FIC
GIL

GRADE 5	LIBRARY MEDIA INSTRUCTIONAL PLAN	DATE_____

Media Coverage

MATERIALS:
5" x 8" Cards and a Marker
Extension Project: Word Search Activity Sheets (see next page) and Pencils

LMC LEARNER STANDARDS

Orientation & Circulation
1. LMC Areas: REVIEW **Circulation Area;** **Fiction/Easy Section(s); Periodical** **Section; Nonfiction Section; Biography** **Section Reference Section; Card/** **Computer Catalog**
2. Vocabulary: REVIEW **media; reference;** **fiction; nonfiction; periodicals; publisher;** **biography; atlas; almanac;** INTRODUCE **audio; visual; classics**
3. REVIEW LMC Rules
4. REVIEW Local Circulation Procedures/ Check Out Books
5. REVIEW Book Care Rules

Literature Appreciation
1. Fiction
   01. Types: Science Fiction; Historical; Realistic
   02. Character; Plot; Setting; Theme
2. Nonfiction
   01. Folklore (Fables, Folktales, Fairy Tales; Tall Tales)
   02. Poetry
   03. Biography
   04. Informational
3. Multicultural Literature
4. Award Books (Newbery; Wilder)
5. Authors/Illustrators

Information Skills
1. Location of Materials: REVIEW/EXTEND Arrangement of Fiction Books; Arrangement of Nonfiction Books; Arrangement of Biography Books; Arrangement of AV Materials
2. Parts of a Book: INTRODUCE **preface &** **copyright page**
3. Research: REVIEW /EXTEND Use of Encyclopedia; Use of Dictionary; Use of Periodicals; Use of Special Reference Books; Use of Atlas; Use of Almanac; Children's Magazine Guide; INTRODUCE Use of Thesaurus
4. Card Catalog: REVIEW/EXTEND 3 Types of Cards & Card Information
5. Dewey Decimal System: INTRODUCE Ten Classes

Technology
1. REVIEW/INTRODUCE Proper Use & Care of Appropriate AV Equipment
2. REVIEW/INTRODUCE Viewing & Listening Skills

CURRICULUM CORRELATION

_____
_____
_____
_____

FOCUS:

Ask the students what they think of when they hear the word *library*. They'll have some cute answers, but someone should say *books*. Ask them why we refer to our library as the *library media center*. Explain that traditionally libraries were storehouses for books, but there is much more than books available in the LMC. Ask students to define the word *media*. *Explain that the various materials that communicate information are called media and today we'll identify the types of media available in the LMC.*

ACTIVITY:

Tell them that books are a kind of media and are called *print media*. Ask students to identify some other types of *print media*. Explain that today we get most of our information from *nonprint media* or *audiovisual materials*. Ask them to recall the definition of *audiovisual* as something you can hear and see. Stress to the students that it is not the *software* or the *equipment* that gives us the information. For example, we can look at a television set all day long, but if there is no program turned on, we've learned nothing. The same is true of computers and even books. Remind the students of the silly goose Petunia in the picture book by Roger Duvoisin. She found a book and carried it around with her all the time thinking it made her really smart, but it wasn't until she caused an accident that she even noticed that there were words on the inside of the book

Have the students look around the LMC and name some media that are available for finding information. All of the following types may not be available in the LMC, but the students should be made aware of them and their uses. In addition, you may have additional types of media available in your LMC.

Books	*Newspapers*	*Magazines*
Vertical File Materials	*Cassettes*	*Computers*
Videotapes	*Microfiche*	*Laserdiscs*
Television	*Transparencies*	*Filmstrips*

Each time the students respond with a type of media that is available in the LMC, write it on a card.

When all the types have been named, divide the students into groups of three or four and hand each group one card listing a kind of media. Give them five minutes to discuss that type of media among themselves and then have each group share with the class a time when one of them was able to learn something using it. It does not have to be for a school assignment. It could have been something they wanted to know for their own benefit.

CLOSURE:

Take the cards back and have the students identify the types of media that have been discussed. Each time something is named, show that card and have one of the students hold it up until all of the types of media have been named. Take the cards back and turn them face down.

EXTENSION:

Explain to the students that you have a word search puzzle for them to do at home and bring back next week. Distribute pencils and the activity sheets and have the students look at the puzzles to see if they have any questions. They should notice immediately that there are no words listed for them to find. Tell them that is their first challenge. They must first identify the types of media. Only ten of them can be found in the puzzle. As a clue, tell the students that of the media discussed today, Vertical File Materials and Laserdiscs are not included in the puzzle. The students may want to jot down the names of some of the media before they leave the LMC while they are still fresh in their memories.

NOTES:

The ten media in the puzzle are: Books, Magazines, Newspapers, Filmstrips, Cassettes, Videotapes, Microfiche, Transparencies, Computers and Television. Make adjustments as needed in the *clues* given to the students.

NAME: _____   CLASS: _____

MEDIA WORD SEARCH

Find the names of ten types of media hidden in the puzzle below. They may be horizontal, vertical or diagonal.

```
M N E W S P A P E R S K B S J A
V I Q M A G A Z I N E S H Y P T
T I C F W N E V M D U L C T K E
A R D R F R I Z Q H Y P G X O L
E V A E O I C O M P U T E R S E
L C T N O F L K B S J A R I Z V
P G X O S T I M F W N E V M D I
C T K B S P A C S J A R I Z Q S
G A X O F W A P H T N E V M B I
C T S K B S J R E E R A R I O O
Y P G S X O F W E S N I E V O N
L C T K E B S J A N R I P Z K X
P G X O F T W N E V C N D S S U
K B S J A R T I Z Q H I Y P G X
N E V M D U L E C T K B E S J A
Q H Y P G X O F S W N E V S M D
```

_____

_____

_____

_____

MEDIA WORD SEARCH
ANSWERS

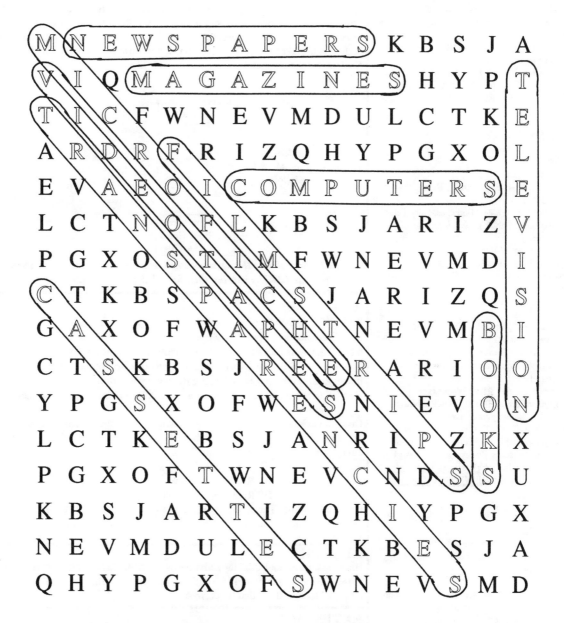

| M | N E W S P A P E R S | K | B | S | J | A |

Books	Newspapers	Computers	Magazines
Television	Microfiche	Cassettes	Videotapes
Filmstrips	Transparencies		

GRADE 6	LIBRARY MEDIA INSTRUCTIONAL PLAN	DATE_____

Circle of Books

LMC LEARNER STANDARDS

Orientation & Circulation
1. LMC Areas: REVIEW **Periodical Section; Circulation Area; Fiction Easy Section(s); Reference Section; Nonfiction Section; Biography Section; Card/Computer Catalog**
2. Vocabulary REVIEW **media; fiction; reference; nonfiction; periodicals; publisher; biography; atlas; audio; visual; classics;** INTRODUCE **autobiography**
3. REVIEW **LMC Rules**
4. REVIEW **Local Circulation Procedures/ Check Out Books**
5. REVIEW **Book Care Rules**

Literature Appreciation
1. Fiction
   01. All Types
   02. Character; Plot; Setting; Theme; Style
2. Nonfiction
   01. Folklore (Fables, Folktales, Fairy Tales; Tall Tales; Mythology & Legends)
   02. Poetry
   03. Biography/Autobiography
3. Multicultural Literature
4. Award Books (Newbery; Carnegie; Coretta Scott King;)
5. Authors/Illustrators

Information Skills
1. Location of Materials: REVIEW/EXTEND Arrangement of Fiction Books; Arrangement of Nonfiction Books; Arrangement of Biography Books & Arrangement of AV Materials
2. Parts of a Book: REVIEW **preface; copyright page;** INTRODUCE **bibliography; footnotes; preface; appendices**
3. Research: REVIEW/EXTEND Use of Encyclopedia; Use of Periodicals; Use of Special Reference Books; Use of Atlas ; Use of Almanac; Use of Thesaurus; Children's Magazine Guide; REINFORCE Outlining for Research
4. Card/Computer Catalog: REVIEW/ EXTEND Types of Cards/Searches & Card/ Record Information
5. Dewey Decimal System: REVIEW/ EXTEND Ten Classes & Recognize Subject of Each

Technology
1. REVIEW/INTRODUCE Proper Use & Care of Appropriate Audiovisual Equipment
2. REVIEW/INTRODUCE Viewing & Listening Skills

CURRICULUM CORRELATION

_____

_____

_____

MATERIALS:
Chalkboard and Chalk or Chart Tablet and Marker
Outline Transparency (see next page), Overhead Projector, Transparency Pens
Extension Project: Paper and Pencils or Pens

FOCUS:
Sixth grade students have been checking out books for several years. Although systems vary from school to school, most students can figure out the steps but they often get confused and leave out a step. Ask the students to define the word *circulation*. (Most of them will define it in terms of the circular path of blood in the body. Try to make the transition from that definition to the use of the term in the LMC. Explain that the circulation of library books is like a circle.)

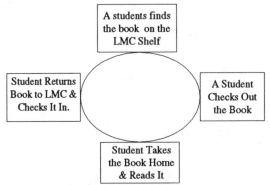

Tell the students that in this lesson we will review the procedure for checking out books from the LMC by sharing their knowledge and outlining the procedures.

ACTIVITY:
Brainstorm with students the things they do when they check out books. Do not worry about sequence at this point. Write all their answers on the chalkboard, or on a chart tablet. (Answers may include: Think about the kind of book wanted; Look in the Card Catalog; Write name on the circulation/book card; Remember to take the book home; Read several pages each night; Remember to return the book on time; Put the circulation/book card back in the book pocket; Return the book to the shelf.)

Once the students have given all their ideas, ask them if these steps could be arranged in groups of related activities. Lead the students to think in terms of four parts of book circulation:
  I. Finding the Book
  II. Borrowing the Book
  III. Reading the Book
  IV. Returning the Book
Using the Outline Transparency, write in the title *Book Circulation*. (Titles will vary.) Write in the four parts above as the main topics on the outline.

CLOSURE:
Have the students look at all the activities listed on the chalkboard or chart tablet. Use those activities as subtopics in the outline. Review the outline and make adjustments until the students think that it's correct.

EXTENSION:
An outline is a guide for writing a composition or report. Have the students use the outline to write a narrative story about a child's adventure with a library book. They must include all of the steps, but they can make the story fun. Suppose a girl checks out a book about magic and disappears. How would the book get back to the LMC? Perhaps a student borrows a biography book and travels back in time to meet that person. This project could be completed in the classroom.

NOTES:
This lesson can be adapted to any circulation system.

Title _____

I. _____

    A. _____

    B. _____

    C. _____

    D. _____

II. _____

    A. _____

    B. _____

    C. _____

    D. _____

III. _____

    A. _____

    B. _____

    C. _____

    D. _____

IV. _____

    A. _____

    B. _____

    C. _____

    D. _____

RESOURCES

Baker, Alan. *Benjamin's Book*. New York: Lothrop, Lee & Shepard Books, 1982. A hamster tries to clean a paw print on the page of his book and only makes matters worse.

Cole, Joanna. *The Clown Arounds*. New York: Parent's Magazine Press, 1981. A family of colorful clowns shows off with silly antics.

Duvoisin, Roger. *Petunia*. New York: Knopf, 1950. A silly goose finds a book and thinks she's instantly intelligent until she learns the hard way that books are only useful to those that can read them.

3 LITERATURE APPRECIATION

In the past several years, the trend in education as been away from textbook teaching toward literature-based learning. Library media specialists have used this technique for many years when presenting lessons on a variety of subjects in the library media center. Suddenly the market is flooded with professional books offering curricular activities based on popular children's books. Students are able to develop an appreciation of quality literature as books are used in the classrooms to teach students concepts that were once limited to textbooks.

Students are also motivated to read and to write once they have been introduced to the authors and illustrators of the books they most enjoy reading. Unfortunately, inviting authors to visit the schools has become very costly. The library media specialist can still excite the students about authors and illustrators by sharing information about them. There are several books available which give brief biographical information about popular authors. Much of the information is written for the students and usually includes personal information and interesting anecdotes. In addition, authors and illustrators often make appearances at bookstores and at library conventions or workshops. Any interesting tidbit of information that the LMS can recall and share with the students will increase their enjoyment of books and reading. Written information from the publisher can be used with photographs and pictures from book covers to create interesting posters about the authors and illustrators. These posters can be displayed in a special location in the library media center.

The literature appreciation lessons in this book do not rely on worksheets, but on oral language experiences and hands-on learning. These lessons provide open-ended learning. In addition to literature appreciation, many of the lessons correlate with other library media learner standards, as well. The titles selected, both fiction and nonfiction, include some well-known contemporary classics as well as some lesser-known titles that may have been overlooked. Outstanding books that reflect cultural pluralism have also been considered. Books used in the lessons are listed in the Resources section at the end of the chapter.

Kindergarten

Beatrix Potter's Animals. Students are introduced to a well-known British author and look at several of her animal characters.

The Tooth Fairy. After listening to a book about the real tooth fairy and a book about stars, students make their own *tooth pouch.*

What's That, Bear? Students can make paper-bag puppets of the various animals in the book, *Brown Bear, Brown Bear, What Do You See?* and participate in the storytelling.

First Grade

Lionni's Fables. After listening to one of Leo Lionni's fables, *Frederick,* students learn how the illustrator creates the little gray mice that are characters in many of his books.

New Year's Wishes. The Sesame Street® characters celebrate New Year's Day through poetry describing their different thoughts about the new year in the book *Sesame Seasons.*

Rain, Rain Go Away. Students vicariously experience a rain storm and share their feelings about rain after listening to the books, *Listen to the Rain* and *Storm in the Night.*

Second Grade

Flutterby Butterfly. Students compare the life cycle of a butterfly in a fiction book, *The Very Hungry Caterpillar* and a nonfiction book, *The Amazing World of Butterflies.*

Life Lines. Students take a look at books of biography by examining several books by Ingri and Edgar D'Aulaire.

Lost in Space. The character Alistair, from the book *Alistair in Outer Space,* inspires the students to return their library books on time.

Third Grade

Caldecott Classification. Students work in pairs to analyze the illustrations in several books which have won the Caldecott Award in order to draw conclusions about the various styles and artistic tecniques used during different time periods.

Greenaway Medal. Students are introduced to several books written by British authors who have won the prestigious Kate Greenaway Medal for their illustrations. A brief description of the award and a list of winners is included.

That Big Bad Wolf. Students re-examine traditional fairy tales which portray the wolf as a villain by looking at *The True Story of the Three Little Pigs* and *The Wolf's Tale* which tell the stories from the wolf's point of view

Fourth Grade

Pollution Solution. After listening to the book *Just a Dream,* students become more aware of their roles in saving the Earth.

Composing Cinquains. Students experience poetry from the poet's view-point in the book, *The Place My Words Are Looking For,* and then create their own poems.

Dual Independence. The Mexican Independence Days, Diez y Seis de Septiembre and Cinco de Mayo are introduced to the students through the book, *Fiesta!* by June Behrens.

Fifth Grade

Beanstalk Sprouts. Students look at the decisions made by the character Jack in the English fairy tale, *Jack and the Beanstalk,* and re-write the ending pretending that Jack made different decisions.

Big Dipper. The Underground Railroad in American history is discussed through the use of the books, *Follow the Drinking Gourd* and *The Drinking Gourd.*

Plot Against a President. After listening to part of the book, *Detective Pinkerton and Mr. Lincoln,* students discover who plotted to assassinate the president in 1860, five years before his death.

Sixth Grade

A Car's Life. After looking at the fictionalized autobiography, *Homesick: My Own Story,* students discuss autobiography as a form of literature.

Cinderella Tales. Students read and compare several *Cinderella* stories from various cultures and write their own modern fairy tale.

Coretta Scott King Award. Students discover Coretta Scott King and the children's book award named after her.

Kindergarten	LIBRARY MEDIA INSTRUCTIONAL PLAN	DATE_____

Beatrix Potter's Animals

LMC LEARNER STANDARDS

Orientation & Circulation
1. LMC Areas: INTRODUCE **Circulation Area; Fiction/Easy Section(s); Periodical Section**
2. Vocabulary: INTRODUCE **LMC; media; author; illustrator; title; fiction**
3. INTRODUCE LMC Rule
4. INTRODUCE Local Circulation Procedures
5. INTRODUCE Book Care Rules

Literature Appreciation
1. Fiction
   01. Types: Picture Books
   02. Elements: Plot (sequence)
2. Nonfiction
   01. Folklore (Fairy Tales; Folktales; Holidays; Nursery Rhymes)
   02. Poetry
3. Multicultural Literature
4. Authors/Illustrators
5. Award Books (Caldecott)

Information Skills
1. Parts of a Book: INTRODUCE **front cover; back cover; title; spine**
2. Research: INTRODUCE Comprehension Skills; Sequencing Skills; Recalling Details; Identifying Main Idea; Alphabetical Order

Technology
1. INTRODUCE Proper Use & Care of Appropriate AV Equipment
2. INTRODUCE Viewing & Listening Skills

CURRICULUM CORRELATION

Science
_____
Art
_____
_____
_____
_____
_____
_____
_____

MATERIALS:
Books, Beatrix Potter's Peter Rabbit: a Lift-the-Flap Book
        Beatrix Potter First Board Books: Dinner Time
        Beatrix Potter First Board Books: Happy Families
        Beatrix Potter First Board Books: Animal Homes
        Beatrix Potter First Board Books: Farmyard Noises
World Map or Atlas
Transparency, "Beatrix Potter's Animals" (see next page)
Overhead Projector, Transparency Pens
Picture of Beatrix Potter
Extension Project: Drawing Paper and Crayons

FOCUS:
Show the students the *Peter Rabbit* book. Most of them will be familiar with Peter. Explain that the person who wrote the story and drew the pictures was named Beatrix Potter. Have the students identify the terms *author* and *illustrator*. Show the students the picture of Beatrix Potter. Explain that she lived in England and wrote The Tale of Peter Rabbit more than 100 years ago. Point out London, England on the map. *Tell the students that we're going to discover more about this author/illustrator and meet some of her animal friends.*

ACTIVITY:
Tell the students that Beatrix Potter lived a lonely life as a child. She lived with her parents and brother in the big city of London, England. Beatrix hated the city and always looked forward to her family's vacations in the countryside. While she was in the country, Beatrix and her brother, Bertram would catch small animals and take them back to the city to keep as pets. They had many pets such as rabbits, frogs, mice, lizards, snakes and even a bat. One of Beatrix's favorite pets, besides Benjamin Bouncer Bunny, was a hedgehog, which is an English animal like a porcupine. Beatrix Potter taught herself to draw and paint and would spend hours painting pictures of her pets. When they died, she'd study their bones so her pictures would look like real animals. Explain that when Beatrix Potter grew up, she moved away from the city and lived on a farm in the countryside where she could be closer to the animals she loved so much. The Tale of Peter Rabbit was Beatrix Potter's first book, but she wrote more than twenty little books about animals. Although the animals in her stories wear clothes, they still look and act a lot like real animals.

Tell the students that we'll look at four books which will tell us a little bit about several animals from many of Beatrix Potter's books. Have them try to remember all the animals that are shown. Read each of the four board books. Have the students recall the various animals in the books.

Show the students the transparency. Tell the students that we will identify the homes, noises, food and babies of each of the animals. Explain that all the answers are not found in the books, so the students will have to rely on what they already know about animals.

CLOSURE:
Show the transparency and complete each column with the help of the students.

EXTENSION:
Tell the students that Beatrix Potter started drawing animals when she was very young and now they're going to get a chance to draw one of her animals, as well. Distribute the drawing paper and crayons. Have the students select different animals and use the crayons to draw them.

NOTES:

Beatrix Potter's Animals

Animal	Home	Noise	Babies	Food
Rabbit				
Mouse				
Frog				
Pig				
Duck				
Chicken				
Cat				
Dog				
Squirrel				

Kindergarten	LIBRARY MEDIA INSTRUCTIONAL PLAN	DATE_____

The Tooth Fairy

LMC LEARNER STANDARDS

Orientation & Circulation
1. LMC Location: INTRODUCE **Circulation Area; Fiction/Easy Section(s); Periodical Section**
2. Vocabulary: INTRODUCE **LMC; media; author; illustrator; title; fiction**
3. INTRODUCE LMC Rules
4. INTRODUCE Local Circulation Procedures
5. INTRODUCE Book Care Rules

Literature Appreciation
1. Fiction
   01. Types: Picture Books
   02. Elements: Plot (sequence)
2. Nonfiction
   01. Folklore (Fairy Tales; Folktales; Holidays; Nursery Rhymes)
   02. Poetry
3. Multicultural Literature
4. Authors/Illustrators
5. Award Books (Caldecott)

Information Skills
1. Parts of a Book: INTRODUCE **front cover; back cover; title; spine**
2. Research: INTRODUCE Comprehension Skills; Sequencing Skills; Recalling Details; Identifying Main Idea; Alphabetical Order

Technology
1. INTRODUCE **Proper Uses & Care of Appropriate AV Equipment**
2. INTRODUCE **Viewing & Listening Skills**

CURRICULUM CORRELATION

Health

MATERIALS:
Book, The Real Tooth Fairy by Marilyn Kaye
Filmstrip, Health Adventures of Lollipop Dragon: Dental Care (SVE)
Filmstrip Projector
Extension Project:
Paper (8" x 11")
Crayons
Glue Stick

FOCUS:
Have the students who have lost some of their baby teeth raise their hands. Discuss why those teeth are called *baby teeth*. Students probably know that new teeth will grow to take the places of the lost teeth. Ask the students what happens to the baby teeth. Lead the discussion toward the idea of a Tooth Fairy. ***Tell the students that today we'll look at a book about the real Tooth Fairy and we'll also discuss how they can take care of their teeth.***

ACTIVITY:
Read the book The Real Tooth Fairy.

Find out if anyone has seen the Tooth Fairy. Have the students recall what the Tooth Fairy in the book looked like. Have them describe the way they think the Tooth Fairy might look.

Have them recall how much money Elise got for her tooth. Ask those students who have lost teeth to recall how much money the Tooth Fairy left them.

Ask the students what the Tooth Fairy in the book did with all the children's teeth after she got them. Have the students think of other things she could do with the teeth.

CLOSURE:
Remind the students that it's very important to take care of their teeth, especially the ones that grow in after their baby teeth fall out. Ask the students to share some things they do to have healthy teeth. Explain that we're going to look at a filmstrip that will tell them how to take care of their teeth.

Show the filmstrip Health Adventures of Lollipop Dragon: Dental Care. Afterwards have the students list the ways to have healthy teeth.

EXTENSION:
The students can make individual Tooth Pouches to put their baby teeth in when they lose them. Give each student a sheet of paper. Have them fold it across the width of the paper, leaving a one-inch strip at the top to form a *flap*. Use the glue stick along the two edges to form an envelope. Have the students write their names on their pouch. Explain that as they lose their baby teeth, they can put them in the pouch where the Tooth Fairy can easily find them. Their parents can even write the date on the outside of the pouch each time a tooth falls out. The students can decorate their Tooth Pouches with stars.

NOTES:

| Kindergarten | **LIBRARY MEDIA INSTRUCTIONAL PLAN** | DATE_____ |

What's That, Bear?

LMC LEARNER STANDARDS

Orientation & Circulation
1. LMC Areas: INTRODUCE **Circulation Area; Fiction/Easy Section(s); Periodical Section**
2. Vocabulary: INTRODUCE **LMC; media, author; illustrator; title; fiction**
3. INTRODUCE LMC Rules
4. INTRODUCE Local Circulation Procedures
5. INTRODUCE Book Care Rules

Literature Appreciation
1. Fiction
   01. Types: Picture Books
   02. Elements: Plot (sequence)
2. Nonfiction
   01. Folklore (Fairy Tales; Folktales; Holidays; Nursery Rhymes)
   02. Poetry
3. Multicultural Literature
4. Authors/Illustrators
5. Award Books (Caldecott)

Information Skills
1. Parts of a Book: INTRODUCE **front cover; back cover; title; spine**
2. Research: INTRODUCE Comprehension Skills; Sequencing Skills; Recalling Details; Identifying Main Idea; Alphabetical Order

Technology
1. INTRODUCE Proper Uses & Care of Appropriate AV Equipment
2. INTRODUCE Viewing & Listening Skills

CURRICULUM CORRELATION

_____

_____

_____

_____

_____

_____

_____

_____

MATERIALS:
Book, Brown Bear, Brown Bear, What Do You See? by Bill Martin, Jr.
Animal Puppets (If time does not allow the students to make their own puppets, make one class set of puppets that you can use with every class.)

Extension Project:
Paper lunch bags
Animal Face Patterns
Crayons, Scissors and Glue

FOCUS:
Have students stand up individually and identify the main color of their clothing. Name the basic eight colors. Teach the students the same eight colors in Spanish. *Tell the students that we'll look at the parts of a book and discover a man who writes books and draws pictures for them.* Show the students the book Brown Bear, Brown Bear, What Do You See? and point out the *front cover, back cover* and *spine* of the book. Some of them may be able to identify the title on the front cover. Point out the title, author and illustrator on the cover of the book. Discuss the meaning of *author, title* and *illustrator*.

ACTIVITY:
Read the book to the class. Explain that you'd like their help in telling the story. Have students recall the various animals in the story. Recall the sequence.

Hand out the puppets and make sure every student has one. There will be several of each animal.

Instruct the students to use their puppets to say the various animals' parts in the story. Read or recite the book again and have the students say their parts. The LMS can take the *teacher* part and the students can be themselves for the part of the children.

CLOSURE:
Have the students recall the names of the animals in the sequence that they appear in the story. They should also be able to recall the title, author and illustrator of the book. Ask them if the pictures look familiar. Some of the students will recognize them as similar to those in other books illustrated by Eric Carle.

EXTENSION:
Using the pictures in the book, or using pictures of animals from a coloring book, draw a pattern for the head of each animal in the book. Only the frontal view of the animal's head is really needed. Let each student color one of the patterns, cut it out and glue it to a bag to make a paperbag puppet.

NOTES:
This is a great activity for bilingual students to have an opportunity to feel good about learning English.

A similar activity can be done using the book Polar Bear, Polar Bear, What Do You Hear? also written by Bill Martin, Jr. and illustrated by Eric Carle.

GRADE 1	LIBRARY MEDIA INSTRUCTIONAL PLAN	DATE_____

Lionni's Fables

LMC LEARNER STANDARDS

Orientation & Circulation
1. LMC Areas: REVIEW **Circulation Area; Fiction/Easy Section(s); Periodical Section**
2. Vocabulary: REVIEW **LMC; media; author; illustrator; title; fiction;** INTRODUCE **spine label; dictionary**
3. REVIEW LMC Rules
4. REVIEW Local Circulation Procedures/ Check Out Books
5. REVIEW Book Care Rules

Literature Appreciation
1. Fiction
   01. Types: Picture Books
   02. Elements: Plot; Character
2. Nonfiction
   01. Folklore (Fairy Tales; Folktales; Holidays; Nursery Rhymes)
   02. Poetry
3. Multicultural Literature
4. Authors/Illustrators
5. Award Books (Caldecott)

Information Skills
1. Location of Materials: INTRODUCE Location of Fiction Books on Shelves by Spine Label
2. Parts of a Book: REVIEW **front cover; back cover; title; spine;** INTRODUCE **title page**
3. Research: REVIEW Comprehension Skills; Sequencing Skills; Recalling Details; Identifying Main Idea; Alphabetical Order; INTRODUCE Identifying Fantasy; Picture Dictionary

Technology
1. REVIEW/INTRODUCE Proper Use & Care of Appropriate AV Equipment
2. REVIEW/INTRODUCE Viewing & Listening Skills

CURRICULUM CORRELATION

Art

_____

_____

_____

_____

_____

MATERIALS:
Videotape, Meet Leo Lionni (American School Publishers)
Books, Frederick by Leo Lionni
   Matthew's Dream by Leo Lionni
   Alexander, the Wind-Up Mouse by Leo Lionni
Globe

Extension Project:
Pattern for Mice (see next page); Black, Pink, Gray and Tan Construction Paper
Black Markers; Glue; Scissors

FOCUS:
Ask the students to define *author* and *illustrator*. Explain that today we'll look at some books by a man who is both the author and the illustrator of his books.
Show the students the books and introduce the author, Leo Lionni. Find Italy on the globe. Explain that Leo Lionni was born in Italy more that 80 years ago and he's old enough to be their great-grandfather. Tell the students that Leo Lionni lives half the year in Italy and the other half in New York. Find New York on the globe. *Tell the students that we will explore Leo Lionni's books and discover how he illustrates them and why he writes his stories.*

ACTIVITY:
Show a few minutes of the videotape so the students can see what Lionni looks like and hear him talk.

Introduce and read the book Frederick. Ask the students why they think Lionni wrote the story. Ask them if there's a *message* in it. Discuss the idea that people need much more than food, homes and clothing to be really happy in life. They need to have pleasure and joy as well.

Have the students look at the pictures of the mice in the story and ask the students to think about how Lionni *drew* the pictures. Explain that he didn't *draw* the mice at all. He *tore* and *cut* them out of pink, black, tan and gray paper and glued the pieces together.

Have the students look carefully at the illustrations as you read the book Matthew's Dream. Ask if they can see how Lionni makes the pictures of the mice. He cuts out the ears, tails, arms and legs, but he tears the bodies to give them a fuzzy look. Ask if they can identify the message of this story. They should see that it's important to know what you want in life and to *go for it!*

If time allows, read and discuss Alexander and the Wind-Up Mouse.

CLOSURE:
Discuss that all of these stories had *messages* or *lessons* from the author. Ask the students if they know of any other famous stories that give lessons. Some of them may know Aesop's Fables. Introduce the word *fable* as a story that teaches a lesson or a moral.

EXTENSION:
Before the lesson, cut out several sets of patterns. Divide the students into groups and give each group a set of patterns, some gray, black, pink, beige and white paper, scissors, glue and markers. Have the students trace the patterns on the correct colors of paper. They may cut out the ears, tails, arms and feet, but they must *tear* around the body. They can glue their *mice* onto paper and draw scenery in the background.

NOTES:
Leo Lionni shared this illustration technique at the Texas Library Association Conference in 1991.

Mouse Pattern

Cut two legs & two arms from black paper.

Cut one ear from pink paper and one ear from
   tan paper.

Cut the tail from pink paper.

Tear the mouse body from gray paper.

The eyes can be made by using the hole punched
   from white paper.

Assemble the mouse just as Leo Lionni does in
   his books.

Use a black marker to finish the eyes and to
   make a nose and whiskers.

| GRADE 1 | **LIBRARY MEDIA INSTRUCTIONAL PLAN** | DATE_____ |

New Year's Wishes

LMC LEARNER STANDARDS

Orientation & Circulation
1. LMC Areas: REVIEW **Circulation Area; Fiction/Easy Section(s); Periodical Section**
2. Vocabulary: REVIEW **LMC; media; author; illustrator; title; fiction;** INTRODUCE **spine label; dictionary**
3. REVIEW LMC Rules
4. REVIEW Local Circulation Procedures/ Check Out Books
5. REVIEW Book Care Rules

Literature Appreciation
1. Fiction
   01. Types: Picture Books
   02. Elements: Plot; Character
2. Nonfiction
   01. Folklore (Fairy Tales; Folktales; Holidays; Nursery Rhymes)
   02. Poetry
3. Multicultural Literature
4. Authors/Illustrators
5. Award Books (Caldecott)

Information Skills
1. Location of Materials: INTRODUCE Location of Fiction Books on Shelves by Spine Label
2. Parts of a Book: REVIEW **front cover; back cover; spine; title;** INTRODUCE **title page**
3. Research: REVIEW Comprehension Skills; Sequencing Skills; Recalling Details; Identifying Main Idea; Alphabetical Order INTRODUCE Identifying Fantasy; Picture Dictionary

Technology
1. REVIEW/INTRODUCE Proper Use & Care of Appropriate AV Equipment
2. REVIEW/INTRODUCE Viewing & Listening Skills

CURRICULUM CORRELATION

_____
_____
_____
_____
_____
_____

MATERIALS:
Book, Sesame Seasons by Linda Haywood
Puppets of Sesame Street® Characters: Big Bird, Oscar, Count
Extension Project:
Book, Gung Hay Fat Chow by June Behrens

FOCUS:
Use the Oscar puppet to welcome the students back to the LMC. Ask the students to identify the current year. Remind them that a new year has just begun. *Explain that people have many different New Year customs. Discuss the word customs. Tell the students that our Sesame Street® friends are going to help us discuss several of these customs.*

ACTIVITY:
Tell the students that Oscar wants to know if they do anything special with their families to celebrate the New Year. Explain that he, like many people, likes to look back at the past year and remember all the good times. Read the poem "Happy New Year from Oscar the Grouch" on page 60 of Sesame Seasons. Have the students recall some of Oscar's memories and let a few of them share some of their own memories of the past year.

Explain that some people don't like to look back at the past. They like to think about the future and how they can have even a better year than last year. They make *resolutions*. Use the Big Bird puppet to read the poem "Big Bird's Poem for New Year's Day" on page 9. Have the students recall some of Big Bird's resolutions and help them make some resolutions of their own.

Explain that the New Year actually starts just after midnight on January 1st, and that sometimes adults have big parties to bring in the New Year. Tell them that kids don't usually go to these parties because they can't stay up that late. Ask the students what they think goes on at these parties right at midnight. Tell them the guests wear party hats, and make a lot of noise with horns and rattles. They make so much noise, they might even wake up their neighbors. Using the Count puppet, show them the picture on page 61 of the Count's New Year's party. Ask the students who the Count would invite to his party. Point out all the bats in the picture. Show the students all the noise makers and the silly hat that one bat is wearing. Explain that they are throwing *confetti* around the room. Ask if any of the students have seen people throwing confetti. Explain that the bats have made such a *ruckus*, that they woke up Bert. Have the students determine the meaning of *ruckus*. Read the poem "Happy New Year from the Count" on page 61.

CLOSURE:
Show the students some hand motions that can accompany the poem.
> They can curl their hands to make a *horn*.
> They can wave their hands above their heads to signify *tassels*.
> They can pretend to throw *confetti* and count it as the pieces fall.
> They can pretend to hold rattles in their hands to shake and bang on imaginary pans.
> They can rub their eyes with their fists to show they've been awakened.
> They can wave their fists in the air and pretend to make a ruckus.

Teach the poem to the students. They can learn it two lines at a time.

EXTENSION:
Explain that some cultures celebrate the New Year on a different day. Show the students the book Gung Hay Fat Chow. Tell the students that the title means *Happy New Year* in Chinese. Explain that Chinese New Year is celebrated in late January or early February each year. Try to find out when it will be celebrated during the current year.

NOTES:

GRADE 1	LIBRARY MEDIA INSTRUCTIONAL PLAN	DATE_____

Rain, Rain, Go Away

LMC LEARNER STANDARDS

Orientation & Circulation
1. LMC Areas: REVIEW **Circulation Area; Fiction/Easy Section(s); Periodical Section**
2. Vocabulary: REVIEW **LMC; media; author; illustrator; title** fiction; INTRODUCE **spine label; dictionary**
3. REVIEW LMC Rules
4. REVIEW Local Circulation Procedures/ Check Out Books
5. REVIEW Book Care Rules

Literature Appreciation
1. Fiction
   01. Types: Picture Books
   02. Elements: Plot; Character
2. Nonfiction
   01. Folklore (Fairy Tales; Folktales; Holidays; Nursery Rhymes)
   02. Poetry
3. Multicultural Literature
4. Authors/Illustrators
5. Award Books (Caldecott)

Information Skills
1. Location of Materials: INTRODUCE Location of Fiction Books on Shelves by Spine Label
2. Parts of a Book: REVIEW **front cover; back cover; spine;** INTRODUCE **title page**
3. Research: REVIEW Comprehension Skills; Sequencing Skills; Recalling Details; Identifying Main Idea; Alphabetical Order; INTRODUCE Identifying Fantasy; Picture Dictionary

Technology
1. REVIEW/INTRODUCE Proper Use & Care of Appropriate AV Equipment
2. REVIEW/INTRODUCE Viewing & Listening Skills

CURRICULUM CORRELATION

Science

_____

_____

_____

_____

_____

MATERIALS:
Book, Listen to the Rain by Bill Martin, Jr.
Book, Storm in the Night by Mary Stolz
Lightweight Cookie Sheet
Prism
Extension Project:
Hot Plate, Pan of Water, Pan of Ice Cubes
Book, The Cloud Book by Tomie dePaola

FOCUS:
Ask the students to share their feelings about rainy days. Have them recall words that describe when it's not raining very hard like *sprinkling, drizzling,* or *misting.* A little heavier rain might be called a rain *shower.* Really heavy rain with thunder and lightning would be a *thunderstorm,* or an *electrical storm.* Ask the students if they have different feelings about rain showers and thunderstorms. *Tell them that we're going to look at two books today that describe kinds of rain and different feelings about rain.*

ACTIVITY:
Introduce the book Listen to the Rain. Point out the author, title and illustrator of the book. Explain that the author uses words so well that we can almost hear the rain. Have the students close their eyes as you read the book. Afterwards ask the students to describe the rain in the first of the story, during the storm and at the end of the story.

Ask if they know how a rainbow appears in the sky after a rainstorm. Briefly explain that, although light around us looks white or clear, it is really many colors mixed together and it takes water or glass or a prism to break the light up so we can see the colors. Show the class the prism and how it makes a rainbow of colors. Explain that raindrops are like tiny prisms and as the light passes through them they divide it into its colors so that we see a rainbow.

Tell the students that we can make the sounds of a rainstorm without any clouds or rain. Divide the students into three groups around you. Demonstrate the effects of *making it rain.* Tap your index fingers together, like you're clapping with them. Add your middle finger to the motion, then your ring finger and your pinkie. Hold your fingers stiffly so that the sound is like a *thud*, not a *clap*. Start out slowly and tap faster and faster. Finally cup your hands and clap quickly and loudly. Have one of the students *flex* the cookie sheet or wave it in the air for a sound like *crackling lightning.* Slow down and reverse the procedure to make the rain stop. Instruct the students that we'll do the same thing in a kind of *round.* Tell them to follow your lead and to start only when you motion to each group. Assign one student to make the *thunder.* After a little practice, this will sound just like a rainstorm. At the end of the *storm,* use the prism to make a *rainbow.*

CLOSURE:
Remind the students that people have different feelings about the rain. If time allows, read the book Storm in the Night and discuss the boy's feelings about the rain.

EXTENSION:
If time allows, or in the classroom, discuss how rain is formed. Show the students the book The Cloud Book and briefly describe the water cycle. Make it *rain* by holding a pan of ice cubes over boiling water. After a few minutes water droplets will form on the bottom of the pan with the ice in it and if the pan is tilted slightly, the *raindrops* will fall from it.

NOTES:
Poetry describing rain might be substituted for the book in the closure portion of the lesson.

GRADE 2	LIBRARY MEDIA INSTRUCTIONAL PLAN	DATE_____

Flutter By, Butterfly

LMC LEARNER STANDARDS

Orientation & Circulation
1. LMC Areas: REVIEW **Circulation Area; Fiction/Easy Section(s); Periodical Section;** INTRODUCE **Reference Section; Nonfiction Section; Biography Section; Card/Computer Catalog**
2. Vocabulary: REVIEW **LMC; media; author; illustrator; title; fiction; spine label; dictionary;** INTRODUCE **biography; nonfiction; table; fairy tale; table of contents; reference; chapter; card catalog**
3. REVIEW LMC Rules
4. REVIEW Local Circulation Procedures/Check Out Books
5. REVIEW Book Care Rules

Literature Appreciation
1. Fiction
   - 01. Types: Realistic; Mystery & Fantasy
   - 02. Elements: Plot; Character; Setting
2. Nonfiction
   - 01. Folklore (Fairy Tales & Fables)
   - 02. Poetry
   - 03. Biography
   - 04. Informational
3. Multicultural Literature
4. Award Books (Caldecott)
5. Authors & Illustrators

Information Skills
1. Location of Materials: REVIEW Arrangement of Fiction Books; INTRODUCE Arrangement of Nonfiction Books & Arrangement of Biography Books
2. Parts of a Book: REVIEW **front cover; back cover; spine; title; title page;** INTRODUCE **table of contents**
3. Research: REVIEW Use of Dictionary; Alphabetical Order; INTRODUCE Use of Maps & Globes; Use of Tables & Graphs; Differences between Books and Periodicals; Differences Between Fact & Fiction

Technology
1. REVIEW/INTRODUCE Proper Use & Care of Appropriate AV Equipment
2. REVIEW/INTRODUCE Viewing & Listening Skills

CURRICULUM CORRELATION

Science
_____
_____
_____
_____
_____
_____

MATERIALS:
Butterfly Puppet
Book, The Very Hungry Caterpillar by Eric Carle
Book, Amazing World of Butterflies and Moths by Louis Sabine
Transparency, "Butterflies and Moths - Comparison/Contrast" (see next page)
Overhead Projector, Transparency Pens
Extension Project: Life Cycle Activity Sheets (see next pages)

FOCUS:
Use the butterfly puppet to welcome the students to the LMC. Ask them to share some *facts* that they've learned in their classroom about butterflies. *Tell the students that we'll take some factual and some fictional looks at butterflies.*

ACTIVITY:
Show them the book The Very Hungry Caterpillar. All of them will have heard it before. Read it to the class and have them read it with you. Ask the students if the book is fiction or nonfiction. They'll know that it's fiction because caterpillars don't eat all those things that the one in the book did. Tell them that we'll investigate butterflies to see if there is something else that makes the book *fiction*.

Ask them if it's true that caterpillars turn into butterflies. They'll say *yes*. Ask if ALL caterpillars turn into butterflies. Some of the students will know that some caterpillars turn into moths. Ask them if butterflies and moths are alike. Tell them that we're going to look at a nonfiction book about butterflies and moths for some true, factual information about how they are alike and how they are different.

Introduce the vocabulary: *hibernate; molting; cocoon; chrysalis; antennae; nectar; proboscis; pupa* and *pupae*). Introduce and read the book Amazing World of Butterflies and Moths.

Have the students share some ways that butterflies and moths are alike and different. Show the Comparison and Contrast Transparency to see if they named all the similarities and differences. (They may have added some.)

Now look at the fiction book The Very Hungry Caterpillar again. As you show each page, discuss what parts of the story are *factual* and which are *imaginary*. The book is not scientifically correct when the butterfly comes from a cocoon in the end of the story. The students may want to know why Eric Carle, the author and illustrator, used a cocoon instead of a chrysalis. Remind the students that fiction books do not have to be factual. They are books of the imagination. The author is able to write the story any way he/she wants to, but nonfiction books must be based on facts.

CLOSURE:
Compare and contrast the fiction book with the nonfiction book. Have the students differentiate between *fiction* and *fact*. Have them describe the ways the two kinds of books are alike and different. Ask if students can always tell if a book is *fiction* or *nonfiction* just by looking at the cover.

EXTENSION:
Distribute the Life Cycle Activity Sheets. Briefly review the stages of the lives of butterflies and moths. Have the students choose a butterfly or a moth and draw pictures of the four stages in the life cycle.

NOTES:
The nonfiction book in this lesson may vary according to the LMC collection. Make sure the appropriate vocabulary words are introduced. The facts on the Comparison/Contrast Transparency were taken from several different books. All of the facts may not be included in the book used in the lesson.

BUTTERFLIES AND MOTHS
COMPARISON AND CONTRAST

Butterflies and Moths are ALIKE because:

They both are hatched from eggs.
They both come from caterpillars.
They're both insects.
They both can fly.
They both have two sets of wings.
They both have scales on their wings.

Butterflies and Moths are DIFFERENT* because:

Their antennae are different. Butterflies have thin straight
    antennae and moths have feathery ones.
Their bodies are different. Butterflies have slender smooth bodies
    and moths have fat hairy bodies.
They hold their wings differently when they're not flying.
    Butterflies hold their wings up together above their bodies
    and moths fold their wings down over their bodies.
They protect their pupae in different ways. Butterflies form a
    chrysalis with the pupa inside and moths build a cocoon or
    burrow into the ground to form their pupae.
They fly at different times. Butterflies fly in the day and moths fly
    at night.
They fly at different speeds. Moths fly faster than butterflies.

*There are some exceptions to these differences.

LIFE CYCLE OF A

_____

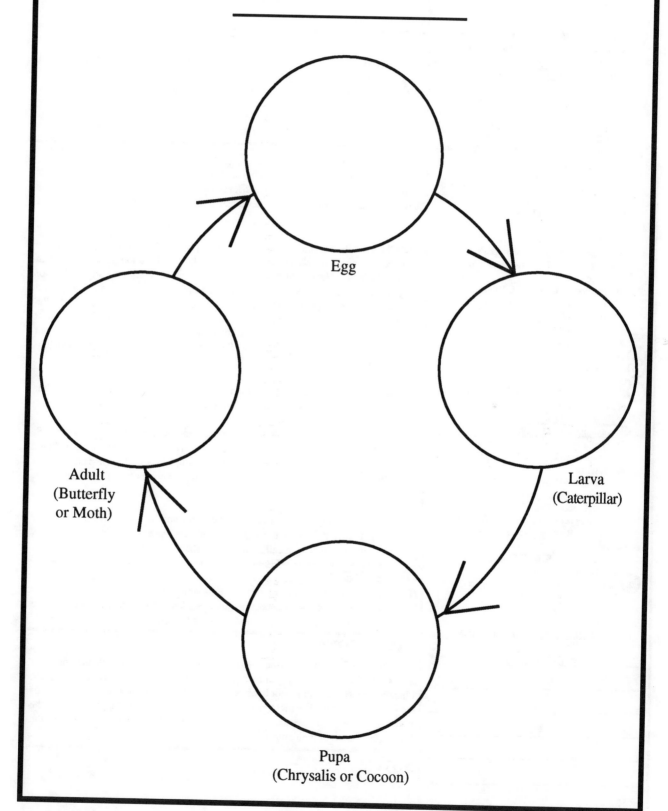

Egg

Larva
(Caterpillar)

Adult
(Butterfly
or Moth)

Pupa
(Chrysalis or Cocoon)

GRADE 2	LIBRARY MEDIA INSTRUCTIONAL PLAN	DATE_____

Life Lines

LMC LEARNER STANDARDS

Orientation & Circulation
1. LMC Areas: REVIEW **Circulation Area; Fiction/Easy Section(s); Periodical Section;** INTRODUCE **Reference Section; Nonfiction Section; Biography Section; Card/Computer Catalog**
2. Vocabulary: REVIEW **LMC; media; author; illustrator; title; fiction; spine label; dictionary;** INTRODUCE **biography; nonfiction; table; fairy tale; table of contents; reference; chapter; card/computer catalog**
3. REVIEW LMC Rules
4. REVIEW Local Circulation Procedures/Check Out Books
5. REVIEW Book Care Rules

Literature Appreciation
1. Fiction
   01. Types: Realistic; Mystery & Fantasy
   02. Elements: Plot; Character; Setting
2. Nonfiction
   01. Folklore (Fairy Tales & Fables)
   02. Poetry
   03. Biography
   04. Informational
3. Multicultural Literature
4. Award Books (Caldecott)
5. Authors & Illustrators

Information Skills
1. Location of Materials: REVIEW Arrangement of Fiction Books; INTRODUCE **Arrangement of Nonfiction Books & Arrangement of Biography Books**
2. Parts of a Book: REVIEW front cover; back cover; spine; **title page;** INTRODUCE **table of contents**
3. Research: REVIEW Use of Dictionary; Alphabetical Order; INTRODUCE Use of Maps & Globes; Use of Tables & Graphs; Differences between Books and Periodicals; Differences Between Fact & Fiction

Technology
1. REVIEW/INTRODUCE Proper Use & Care of Appropriate AV Equipment
2. REVIEW/INTRODUCE Viewing & Listening Skills

CURRICULUM CORRELATION

Social Studies

_____

_____

_____

_____

_____

MATERIALS:
Filmstrip, Biography (Pied Piper); Filmstrip Projector
Several biography books by Ingri and Edgar D'Aulaire.
Enlarged spine labels of biographies used in the lesson (Make these on 5" x 8" cards)
Chalk and Chalkboard or Vocabulary Board

FOCUS:
Have students define *nonfiction*. Explain that there are some special true, informational books which are books about people and their lives. (Be careful about using the term *story* here because students may associate *story* with a fictional story book.) Introduce the term *biography* by writing it on the chalkboard or pointing it out on the vocabulary board. ***Tell the students that today we'll discover exactly what biography books are and where we can find them in the LMC.***

ACTIVITY:
Introduce the filmstrip. It discusses the book about Ben Franklin by Ingri and Edgar D'Aulaire. Instruct the students to watch for at least five of Franklin's accomplishments that affect our lives today. Show the filmstrip and have the students name some of Franklin's contributions.

Show the book Benjamin Franklin. Look at the spine label on the book. Hold up the enlarged version so that students can clearly see the classification (it may vary from school to school). Have them identify the differences between the call numbers of Biography, Fiction and Nonfiction. Look at the bottom part of the call number and show students that biographies of individuals are shelved in alphabetical order by the person the book is about, not by the author. This makes biographies some of the easiest books to find on the shelves. Just think about the last name of the person you want to know about. Then go to the Biography Section of the LMC and look alphabetically through the books for that name.

Have the students point out the Biography Section of the LMC. Find several other biographies by the D'Aulaires from the shelves and show them to the class.

Find a collective biography book on the shelves (one about the Presidents of the U.S. is a good choice) and show it to the students. Discuss that the book includes information about several people. Ask how they would decide which last name to use for shelving this book. (They'll have lots of good answers for which you need great responses.)

Explain the meaning of *collective biography* and how it differs from *individual biography*. Point out that *collection* means *more than one* and *individual* means *one*. Also show the differences in call numbers and shelf arrangement.

CLOSURE:
Have selected students re-shelve the various biography books used during the lesson in their proper places while the remaining students direct them. Review the definitions of *individual biography* and *collective biography*.

EXTENSION:
Talk about the D'Aulaires and their artistic techniques. They have both died, but their books are still used and enjoyed by children today. One of their books, Abraham Lincoln, was a Caldecott Honor book. Ask students to recall how an illustrator wins the Caldecott Medal. The pictures in the books are called lithographs. Also tell the students that the D'Aulaires did a lot of research to write their books. They visited the places where each of their subjects lived and worked.

NOTES:

| GRADE 2 | **LIBRARY MEDIA INSTRUCTIONAL PLAN** | DATE_____ |

Lost in Space

LMC LEARNER STANDARDS

Orientation & Circulation
1. LMC Areas: REVIEW **Circulation Area; Fiction/Easy Section(s); Periodical Section;** INTRODUCE **Reference Section; Nonfiction Section; Biography Section; Card/Computer Catalog**
2. Vocabulary: REVIEW **LMC; media; author; illustrator; title; fiction; spine label; dictionary;** INTRODUCE **biography; nonfiction; fable; fairy tale; table of contents; reference; chapter; card/ computer catalog**
3. REVIEW LMC Rules
4. REVIEW Local Circulation Procedures/ Check Out Books
5. REVIEW Book Care Rules

Literature Appreciation
1. Fiction
   01. Types: Realistic; Mystery & Fantasy
   02. Elements: Plot; Character; Setting
2. Nonfiction
   01. Folklore (Fairy Tales & Fables)
   02. Poetry
   03. Biography
   04. Informational
3. Multicultural Literature
4. Award Books (Caldecott)
5. Authors & Illustrators

Information Skills
1. Location of Materials: REVIEW Arrangement of Fiction Books; INTRODUCE Arrangement of Nonfiction Books & Arrangement of Biography Books
2. Parts of a Book: REVIEW **title page;** INTRODUCE **table of contents**
3. Research: REVIEW Use of Dictionary; Alphabetical Order; INTRODUCE Use of Maps & Globes; Use of Tables & Graphs; Differences between Books and Periodicals; Differences Between Fact & Fiction

Technology
1. REVIEW/INTRODUCE Proper Use & Care of Appropriate AV Equipment
2. REVIEW/INTRODUCE Viewing & Listening Skills

CURRICULUM CORRELATION

_____

_____

_____

_____

_____

MATERIALS:
Poster of LMC Rules
World Map or Atlas
Book, Alistair in Outer Space by Marilyn Sadler
Vocabulary Cards, *Character; Setting; Plot*
Transparency "Elements of Fiction" (see next page)
Overhead Projector, Transparency Pens
Extension Project: Bookmarks (see next pages)

FOCUS:
Have the students recall the various rules of Library Media Center. Point out the rule about returning library books on time. Discuss the meaning of *on time*. Ask students why this rule is important. Most of them will be able to recall a time when they wanted certain books which were checked out by other students. They can identify with the *agony* of having to wait for the book each week as the other student forgot to return it. Ask the students to recall some excuses students often give for forgetting to return their books to the LMC on time. *Tell the students that today we'll review the rules of the LMC, especially the one about returning library books on time.*

ACTIVITY:
Tell the students that today they'll meet a book *character* who always returned his library books on time. Hold up the word *character* as you say it. Show the book Alistair in Outer Space to the class and point out Alistair. Tell the class the *setting* of the story is your town or city. Hold up the word *setting* as you say it. Point out your town or city on a world map or atlas. Tell the class that a strange thing happened to Alistair when he was on his way to return his books to the library. Tell the students to listen carefully to the *plot* of the story so they'll know what happened to Alistair. Hold up the word *plot* as you say it.

Read the book. At the end of the story have the students identify Antarctica as the place where Alistair landed. (Some students may argue that he landed at the North Pole. Tell those *wisecrackers* that Santa is not in the picture and, besides that, penguins live only at the South Pole, not at the North Pole.) Find Antarctica on the map or in the atlas. Ask the students if they think Alistair will get to the library before it closes. It looks like his books will be late for the first time.

Tell the students that we'll look at the elements of the story. Use the transparency and have the students identify the *characters, setting* and *plot* of the story. Point out that the story is definitely *fiction*.

CLOSURE:
Remind the students that everyone, including Alistair, will forget to return a library book at one time or another, but like Alistair, they must try their best to remember to return their books on time because someone else may be waiting to borrow them.

EXTENSION:
Tell the students that perhaps having special bookmarks would help them remember to return their library books on time. Photocopy and cut out enough bookmarks so that each child can have one. Distribute the bookmarks and read the poem. Have them write their names at the top of the bookmark and the day of the week that their class comes to the LMC at the bottom.

NOTES:
Marilyn Sadler has written several adventures about Alistair:
Alistair's Elephant
Alistair Underwater
Alistair's Time Machine

ELEMENTS OF FICTION

Character(s)
(The animals or people in the story)

Setting
(Where the story takes place)

Plot
(What happens in the story)

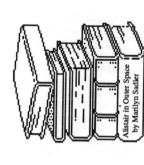
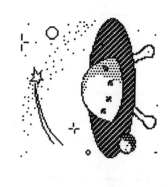

Watch Out for Spaceships in the Air!

Don't let those Creatures capture YOU!

Just think of little Alistair,

and return your books when they're DUE!

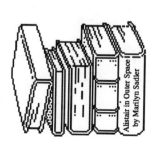

Alistair in Outer Space
by Marilyn Sadler

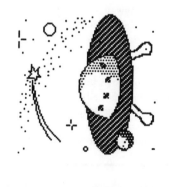

Watch Out for Spaceships in the Air!

Don't let those Creatures capture YOU!

Just think of little Alistair,

and return your books when they're DUE!

Alistair in Outer Space
by Marilyn Sadler

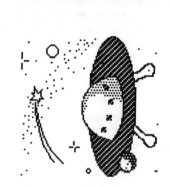

Watch Out for Spaceships in the Air!

Don't let those Creatures capture YOU!

Just think of little Alistair,

and return your books when they're DUE!

Alistair in Outer Space
by Marilyn Sadler

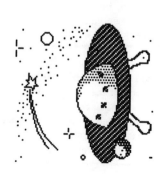

Watch Out for Spaceships in the Air!

Don't let those Creatures capture YOU!

Just think of little Alistair,

and return your books when they're DUE!

Alistair in Outer Space
by Marilyn Sadler

GRADE 3	LIBRARY MEDIA INSTRUCTIONAL PLAN	DATE_____

Caldecott Classification

LMC LEARNER STANDARDS

Orientation & Circulation
1. LMC Areas: REVIEW **Circulation Area; Fiction/Easy Section(s); Periodical Section; Reference Section; Card/Computer Catalog; Nonfiction Section; Biography Section**
2. Vocabulary: REVIEW **media; reference; fiction; nonfiction; periodicals; chapter;** INTRODUCE **publisher; call number; almanac; copyright date; atlas**
3. REVIEW LMC Rules
4. REVIEW Local Circulation Procedures/ Check Out Books
5. REVIEW Book Care Rules

Literature Appreciation
1. Fiction
   01. Types: Mystery; Realistic
   02. Elements: Plot; Character & Setting
2. Nonfiction
   01. Folklore (Fables, Folktales, Fairy Tales)
   02. Poetry
   03. Biography
   04. Informational
3. Multicultural Literature
4. Authors/Illustrators
5. Award Books (Caldecott, Greenaway)

Information Skills
1. Location of Materials: REVIEW/EXTEND Arrangement of Fiction Books; Arrangement of Nonfiction Books & Arrangement of Biography Books
2. Parts of a Book: REVIEW **table of contents, title page;** INTRODUCE **glossary; index**
3. Research: REVIEW /EXTEND Use of Dictionary; Alphabetical Order; INTRODUCE Use of Encyclopedia; Use of Periodicals; Use of Special Reference Books; Use of Atlas
4. Card/Computer Catalog: INTRODUCE Types of Cards/Searches & Card/Record Information

Technology
1. REVIEW /INTRODUCE Proper Use & Care of Appropriate AV Equipment
2. REVIEW /INTRODUCE Viewing & Listening Skills

CURRICULUM CORRELATION

Art

MATERIALS:
10 or 15 books that have been awarded the Caldecott Medal (Silver or Gold)
    (Make sure the books selected display a variety of art techniques)
Sticky Notes (Place one on the front cover of each book); Pencils
A poster or book listing the *Caldecott Books*

FOCUS:
Remind the students that they have been learning about the Caldecott Medal which is awarded annually to an illustrator for the book with the most outstanding illustrations published in the previous year. *Explain that we will examine several of those books and draw some conclusions about the kinds of artwork in the books.*

ACTIVITY:
Have each student select a partner and give each pair of students one of the *Caldecott* books and a pencil. Tell the students to number from 1 to 5 on the note. Remind them to write *lightly*. Explain that the students will analyze the their books by answering questions about them. Ask the following questions and have the students write the answers by the numbers on the notes.

    1. Have the students look on the back of the title pages to find the dates their books were first published. Have them add one year to that date and write the answer on their notes. Walk around and make sure the students are able to locate the correct date. Many of these books have been reprinted several times.

    2. Have the students check to see if the illustrators of their books were also the authors. Have them write *yes* or *no* for an answer.

    3. Have the students look to find out how many colors were used by the illustrators. Have them write *few* or *many* for the answer.

    4. Discuss the *style* of the pictures. Talk about cartoon-like drawings as opposed to realistic drawings. Have the students decide which style they think the pictures in their books are and record their answers on the notes.

    5. Have the students determine the kind of *medium* the illustrator used–colored pencil, pen and ink, watercolors, oil paint, woodcuts, etc. The students will not have much background, but let them write an answer anyway.

    Now the students are ready for comparisons and conclusions. Verify the year that each student's book won the award by checking the poster or book listing the Caldecott winners. Have the students with books that won the award before 1950 stand on one side of the room and those with later books stand on the other side. Have the students hold the books open showing some of the pictures. Help the students determine if books winning the award before or after 1950 had more colorful pictures. Have the students raise their hands if the illustrators of their books were also the authors. Determine if, more often than not, the illustrator was also the author of the book. Identify and compare the styles and techniques of the pictures to determine that they are varied.

CLOSURE:
Have the students summarize their conclusions about the books that have won the Caldecott Award. Answers might include: Newer books have more colorful pictures most of the time; many times the author is also the illustrator; many styles and techniques are used. Explain that we only looked a sampling of the winners, so we cannot say that these conclusions apply to all the books.

EXTENSION:
If time allows tell the students that one important aspect of a book's illustrations is that the pictures coordinate with the tone or mood of the story. For instance, if Stephen Gammell had used hot pink and white instead of black and white to illustrate Where the Buffaloes Begin, it might not have been selected as an honor book because it is a serious quiet book about Native Americans. Also, the navy ink used in Blueberries for Sal was perfect for that book, but not for every book.

NOTES:
Cooperative learning is the key to this lesson.

GRADE 3	LIBRARY MEDIA INSTRUCTIONAL PLAN	DATE_____

Greenaway Medal

LMC LEARNER STANDARDS

Orientation & Circulation
1. LMC Areas: REVIEW **Circulation Area;
   Fiction/Easy Section(s); Periodical Section;
   Reference Section; Nonfiction Section;
   Biography Section; Card/Computer Catalog**
2. Vocabulary: REVIEW **media; reference;
   fiction; nonfiction; periodicals; chapter;**
   INTRODUCE **publisher; call number;
   almanac; copyright date; atlas**
3. REVIEW LMC Rules
4. REVIEW Local Circulation Procedures/
   Check Out Books
5. REVIEW Book Care Rules

Literature Appreciation
1. Fiction
   01. Types: Mystery; Realistic
   02. Elements: Plot; Character & Setting
2. Nonfiction
   01. Folklore (Fables, Folktales, Fairy Tales)
   02. Poetry
   03. Biography
   04. Informational
3. Multicultural Literature
4. Authors/Illustrators
5. Award Books (Caldecott; Greenaway)

Information Skills
1. Location of Materials: REVIEW/EXTEND
   Arrangement of Fiction Books; Arrangement
   of Nonfiction Books & Arrangement of
   Biography Books
2. Parts of a Book: REVIEW **table of contents,
   title page;** INTRODUCE **glossary; index**
3. Research: REVIEW /EXTEND Use of
   Dictionary; Alphabetical Order; INTRODUCE
   Use of Encyclopedia; Use of Periodicals; Use
   of Special Reference Books; Use of Atlas
4. Card/Computer Catalog: INTRODUCE Types
   of Cards/Searches & Card/Record Information

Technology
1. REVIEW /INTRODUCE Proper Use & Care
   of Appropriate AV Equipment
2. REVIEW /INTRODUCE Viewing &
   Listening Skills

CURRICULUM CORRELATION

Art

_____

_____

_____

_____

_____

_____

MATERIALS:
Filmstrip, <u>Charley, Charlotte and the Golden Canary</u> (Weston Woods); Projector
World Map, Atlas or Globe
Book, <u>Wind Blew</u> by Pat Hutchins
Book, <u>Mr. Gumpy's Outing</u> by John Burningham
Book, <u>Meet the Authors and Illustrators</u> by Deborah Kovacs and James Preller
Books Illustrated by Kate Greenaway: <u>Under the Window</u> and <u>A Apple Pie</u>
Extension Project:
Picture Tags of the animals in the book, <u>Mr. Gumpy's Outing</u> (Using a coloring book
   or a book of clip art, find pictures of each of the animals in the story. Draw the
   animals on tagboard and tie yarn to the top of the pictures so the students can hang
   them around their necks.)
Straw Hat; Baseball Cap and Hair Bow

FOCUS:
Ask the students to identify *illustrator*. Ask them what award is given to the American
illustrator for the best picture book each year. Stress that the Caldecott Award is given
only to illustrators living in America. Ask if the students know who the award is
named for. Have them recall some books that have won the Caldecott Medal. Explain
that other countries give book awards also. Show them Britain on the map, atlas or
globe. *Explain that the British Library Association also gives an award for the most
distinguished picture book published in Britain each year. It's called the Kate
Greenaway Medal. Tell the students that we're going to look at some of the books
that have won the award.*

ACTIVITY:
Show and discuss the filmstrip <u>Charley, Charlotte and the Golden Canary</u>. Remind
the students to look carefully at the pictures because the illustrator won the award for
his drawings.

Introduce the book <u>The Wind Blew</u>. Ask the students if they can recall any other books
by Pat Hutchins. Read the book. Look at the pictures carefully and have the students
compare them with those in the filmstrip. Read the profile of Pat Hutchins in the book
<u>Meet the Authors and Illustrators</u>.

Introduce the book <u>Mr. Gumpy's Outing</u>. Explain that in England the people speak
English, but it's different from the English spoken in America. Introduce the
following vocabulary: *outing; squabble; muck; bleat; tramp.* Show the cover of the
book and ask the student where they think Mr. Gumpy's outing will be. Have them
identify some of the *friends* that he's taking with him and predict the outcome of taking
so many animals on a boat together. Read the book.

CLOSURE:
Have the students recall the name of the picture book award given in Britain. Ask them
who they think the person Kate Greenaway might have been. Have a student look up
Kate Greenaway in the encyclopedia and read the entry to the class. Show the books
illustrated by Greenaway and discuss why a picture book award would be named after
her.

EXTENSION:
Have the students act out the story of <u>Mr. Gumpy's Outing</u>. Have a student be Mr.
Gumpy and wear the straw hat. The student playing the boy can wear the baseball cap
and the girl can wear the bow in her hair. The students acting the parts of the animals
can wear the *tags*. The remaining students will join hands and form a circle which will
be the *boat*. Read the story and have the students practice their parts. Then read the
story slowly while they act it out.

NOTES:
This lesson can be shortened to take only one class session by including only two
books, but if possible, spend a little extra time on this subject. The Greenaway Medal
is not given very much attention in this country.

The Kate Greenaway Medal

The Greenaway Medal is named in honor of Catherine Greenaway (1846-1901), a noted English author and illustrator of books for children. Kate Greenaway, along with Randolph Caldecott (who was also born in England in the same year as Greenaway) helped to bring about important changes in children's literature. Her drawings portrayed happy children in colorful, playful settings and her books were some of the first written for the purpose of bringing pleasure to children, rather than teaching morals.

The award was established in 1955 by the Library Association (British) and the first medal was give in 1957. A selection committee of thirteen Library Association (British) members makes the final selection, but nominations are accepted from the membership in general. The Greenaway Medal is awarded annually to the <u>illustrator</u> of an outstanding book published in the United Kingdom during the previous year. Most of the time, several other books are listed as <u>Highly Commended</u> and <u>Commended.</u>

The committee considers several criteria, including the following:
- Artistic Merit, including design, format and production
- Imaginative and Complementary Interpretation of the Text
- Graphic Style and Consistency
- Appeal to Children's Perceptions
- Style and Layout of Illustrations in Relation to the Text
- Appropriate Interpretation of Character and Theme

Winners of the Kate Greenaway Medal

1957 - <u>Tim all Alone</u>, written & illustrated by Edward Ardizzone

1958 - <u>Mrs. Easter and the Storks</u>, written & illustrated by Violet Hilda Drummond

1960 - <u>Bundle of Ballads</u> , compiled by Ruth Manning-Sanders; Illustrated by William Stobbs

1961 - <u>Old Winkle and the Seagulls</u> by Elizabeth Rose; illustrated by Gerald Rose

1963 - <u>Brian Wildsmith's ABC</u>, written & illustrated by Brian Wildsmith

1964 - <u>Borka, the Adventures of a Goose with No Feathers</u>, written & illustrated by John Burningham

1965 - *Shakespeare's Theatre*, written & illustrated by C. Walter Hodges
1966 - *Three Poor Tailors*, written & illustrated by Victor Ambrus
1967 - *Mother Goose Treasury*, written & illustrated by Raymond Briggs
1968 - *Charley, Charlotte and the Golden Canary*, written & illustrated by Charles Keeping
1969 - *Dictionary of Chivalry* by Grant Uden; illustrated by Pauline Baynes
1970 - *Dragon of an Ordinary Family* by Margaret Mahy; illustrated by Helen Oxenbury
1971 - *Mr. Gumpy's Outing*, written & illustrated by John Burningham
1972 - *Kingdom Under the Sea,* written & illustated by Jan Pienkowski
1973 - *Woodcutter's Duck,* written & illustrated by Krystyna Turska
1974 - *Father Christmas*, written & illustrated by Raymond Briggs
1975 - *Wind Blew,* written & illustrated by Pat Hutchins
1976 - *Horses in Battle*, written & illustrated by Victor Ambrus
1977 - *Post Office Cat*, written & illustrated by Gail Haley
1978 - *Dogger*, written & illustrated by Shirley Hughes
1979 - *Each Peach, Pear, Plum*, written & illustrated by Janet & Allan Ahlberg
1980 - *Haunted House*, written & illustrated by Jan Pienkowski
1981 - *Mr. Magnolia*, written & illustrated by Quentin Blake
1982 - *Highwayman* by Alfred Noyes; illustrated by Charles Keeping
1983 - *Long Neck and Thunderfoot* by Helen Piers; illustrated by Michael Foreman
1984 - *Gorilla* , written & illustrated by Anthony Browne
1985 - *Hiawatha's Childhood*, by Henry Wadsworth Longfellow; illustrated by Errol LeCain
1986 - *Sir Gawain and the Loathly Lady* by Selina Hastings; illustrated by Juan Wijngaard
1987 - *Snow White in New York*, written & illustrated by Fiona French
1988 - *Crafty Chameleon* by Mwenye Hadithi; illustrated by Adrienne Kennaway
1989 - *Can't You Sleep, Little Bear*, written & illustrated by Martin Waddell & Barbara Firth
1990 - *War Boy: a Country Childhood*, written & illustrated by Michael Foreman
1991 - *Whales' Song* by Dyan Sheldon; illustrated by Gary Blythe
1992 - *Jolly Christmas Postman* written & illustrated by Janet & Allan Ahlberg

GRADE 3	**LIBRARY MEDIA INSTRUCTIONAL PLAN**	**DATE**_____

That Big Bad Wolf

LMC LEARNER STANDARDS

Orientation & Circulation
1. LMC Areas: REVIEW **Circulation Area; Fiction/Easy Section(s); Periodical Section; Reference Section; Nonfiction Section; Biography Section; Card/Computer Catalog**
2. Vocabulary: REVIEW **media; reference; fiction; nonfiction; periodicals; chapter;** INTRODUCE **publisher; call number; almanac; copyright date; atlas**
3. REVIEW LMC Rules
4. REVIEW Local Circulation Procedures/ Check Out Books
5. REVIEW Book Care Rules

Literature Appreciation
1. Fiction
   01. Types: Mystery; Realistic
   02. Elements: Plot; Character & Setting
2. Nonfiction
   01. Folklore (Fables, Folktales, Fairy Tales)
   02. Poetry
   03. Biography
   04. Informational
3. Multicultural Literature
4. Authors/Illustrators
5. Award Books (Caldecott, Greenaway)

Information Skills
1. Location of Materials: REVIEW /EXTEND Arrangement of Fiction Books; Arrangement of Nonfiction Books & Arrangement of Biography Books
2. Parts of a Book: REVIEW **table of contents, title page;** INTRODUCE **glossary; index**
3. Research: REVIEW/EXTEND Use of Dictionary; Alphabetical Order INTRODUCE Use of Encyclopedia; Use of Periodicals; Use of Special Reference Books; Use of Atlas
4. Card Catalog/Computer: INTRODUCE Types of Cards/Searches & Card/Record Information

Technology
1. REVIEW /INTRODUCE Proper Use & Care of Appropriate AV Equipment
2. REVIEW /INTRODUCE Viewing & Listening Skills

CURRICULUM CORRELATION

_____

_____

_____

_____

_____

MATERIALS:
Book, The Jolly Postman by Janet and Allan Ahlberg
Book, The True Story of the Three Little Pigs by Jon Scieszka
Book, Little Red Riding Hood/The Wolf's Tale (Upside Down Tales) by Della Rowland
Extension Project:
Story, "The Wolf and the Seven Little Kids" (available in The Arbuthnot Anthology of Children's Literature by May Hill Arbuthnot)

FOCUS:
Ask the students to recall their favorite fairy tales. Have them imagine a Fairy Tale Land where all the characters live together. Show them the book The Jolly Postman and introduce it as a book of letters that the residents of Fairy Tale Land have sent each other. Read the letter from the Three Pigs' attorney to B.B. Wolf. *Tell the students that we will take another look at some fairy tales to see if perhaps there's another side to the story.*

ACTIVITY:
Look at the letter from the Three Pigs' attorney again. Suggest that maybe those pigs were not so defenseless or innocent as the original story portrayed them. Tell the students that maybe there was another side of the story and that maybe the wolf was innocent. Introduce and read the book The True Story of the Three Little Pigs.

Remind the students that the wolf is a villain in many fairy tales. Ask them to recall the story of Little Red Riding Hood. She, too, was an innocent victim of the big, bad wolf who ate up her granny and tried to eat her too. Of course, even that story could have another side. Show the students the Upside Down Tale book Little Red Riding Hood. Flip the book over and read The Wolf's Tale.

Afterwards, have the students divide into two groups. In one group will be the students who believe that the wolf is guilty and in the other will be students who believe he is innocent. Give the students about five minutes to discuss the issues within the groups. Each group will pick a speaker who will defend the group's verdict to the class.

CLOSURE:
Some of the students may change their minds after hearing all of the groups' discussions. Take a final vote to determine if the class finds the wolf guilty or innocent of his crimes in Fairy Tale Land. If he is found guilty, discuss a proper sentence. If he is innocent, discuss the reparations that should be made to clear his name.

Remind the students that the original stories are fairy tales and are located in the 300 section of the nonfiction books. The new versions, however are fiction and will be located in the Fiction Section of the LMC, probably with the picture books.

EXTENSION:
Read the story "The Wolf and the Seven Little Kids." Have the students take the wolf's side and make up a new version of the story. This could also be done as a writing assignment in the classroom.

NOTES:
There is a sequel to The Jolly Postman, The Jolly Christmas Postman, in which the wolf sends a letter to Little Red Riding Hood.

Jon Scieszka has written another book, The Frog Prince Continued, in which he explains what happened to the Frog Prince and the Princess after they were destined to *live happily ever after!*

GRADE 4	LIBRARY MEDIA INSTRUCTIONAL PLAN	DATE_____

Pollution Solution

LMC LEARNER STANDARDS

Orientation & Circulation
1. LMC Areas: REVIEW **Circulation Area; Fiction/Easy Section(s); Periodical Section; Reference Section; Nonfiction Section; Biography Section; Card/Computer Catalog**
2. Vocabulary: REVIEW **media; reference; fiction; nonfiction; periodicals; publisher; biography; atlas; almanac; call number; copyright date;** INTRODUCE **unabridged dictionary; thesaurus; verso**
3. REVIEW LMC Rules
4. REVIEW Local Circulation Procedures/ Check Out Books
5. REVIEW Book Care Rules

Literature Appreciation
1. Fiction
   01. Types: Historical, Realistic; Humorous; Adventure
   02. Elements: Character; Plot; Setting
2. Nonfiction
   01. Folklore (Fables, Folktales, Fairy Tales)
   02. Poetry
   03. Biography
   04. Informational
3. Multicultural Literature
4. Authors/Illustrators
5. Award Books (Newbery; Coretta Scott King)

Information Skills
1. Location of Materials: REVIEW / EXTEND Arrangement of Fiction Books; Arrangement of Nonfiction Books & Arrangement of Biography Books; INTRODUCE Arrangement of Audiovisual Materials
2. Parts of a Book: REVIEW **table of contents; title page; glossary, index;** INTRODUCE **dedication**
3. Research: REVIEW/EXTEND Alphabetical Order; Use of the Encyclopedia; Use of the Dictionary; Use of Periodicals; Use of Special Reference Books ; INTRODUCE Use of Atlas; Use of Almanac; Children's Magazine Guide
4. Card/Computer Catalog: REVIEW /EXTEND Types of Cards/Searches & Card/Record Information

Technology
1. REVIEW/INTRODUCE Proper Use & Care of Appropriate AV Equipment & Software
2. REVIEW/INTRODUCE Viewing & Listening Skills

CURRICULUM CORRELATION
Science

_____

_____

_____

_____

MATERIALS:
Lots of Trash
An Aquarium or Terrarium Filled with Dirt
Book, Just a Dream by Chris Van Allsburg
Extension Project:
Pencil and Paper for Writing Student Responses

FOCUS:
Before the class comes in, write the vocabulary words *ecology, conservation, pollution , recycle* and *biodegradable* on pieces of paper. Crumple the paper up and scatter around the LMC, along with an empty aluminum can, a styrofoam cup, a pencil, some newspaper, a toilet paper roll, aluminum foil, a plastic grocery bag and any other trash you have about. Toss it on the floor where the students will have to walk around it to get in. Notice if anyone picks up any of the trash. After the students are seated in the LMC, tell them that we're going to clean up a little bit. Have them pick up the trash from the floor and hold it their hands or stack it on their table. Have the students open the trash paper and find and discuss the vocabulary words that appear on some of the trash. *Explain that they'll listen to a book which should make them think about the future of our planet and the consequences of a careless lack of conservation.*

ACTIVITY:
Remind the students that although everyone is aware of the pollution problem that we have in our world today, many people are unconcerned.

Read the book Just a Dream.

Remind students that in addition to more trees, our world needs less trash. Discuss what happens to the trash we constantly make. Have students recount the trash they have already made that day. Ask them the following questions:
What did you have for breakfast? Did it have a paper or plastic wrapper? Did you use a paper plate or napkin? How much notebook paper have you wasted already? Did you break a pencil and throw it away? Did you get a ride to school? Did you bring a lunch in a paper bag? They will be able to think of many ways they have inadvertently polluted the planet. Discuss where the trash is taken when it is picked up.

Have the students look at the trash they have collected in the LMC. Ask them which items they think will decompose in the soil.

CLOSURE:
Have the students bury the objects in the dirt that you have provided in a large aquarium. Label each item. This will be their laboratory for an ecology experiment. Several months later, excavate the dirt to discover which items have begun to decompose and which have not.

EXTENSION:
Remind the students that once Walter, the boy in Just a Dream became aware of how his actions were affecting the environment, he changed his behavior and thus changed the future. Students will quickly be able to list all the things they can do to *save the Earth*, but they do not always practice these good habits. After the students list their Earth-saving tips, make a class list and type it on a sheet of paper. Distribute copies to the students and instruct them to tape the lists to their bedroom doors. Tell the students to check the list each Saturday and mark each thing they've done that week. At the same time you excavate the trash pile, have the students bring in their lists and share their efforts with the class.

NOTES:
There are many books currently being written on this topic that could be worked into the lesson if they are available in the LMC collection and if time allows.

GRADE 4	LIBRARY MEDIA INSTRUCTIONAL PLAN	DATE_____

Composing Cinquains

LMC LEARNER STANDARDS

Orientation & Circulation
1. LMC Areas: REVIEW **Circulation Area; Fiction/Easy Section(s); Periodical Section; Reference Section; Nonfiction Section; Biography Section; Card/Computer Catalog**
2. Vocabulary: REVIEW **media; reference; fiction; nonfiction; periodicals; publisher; biography; atlas; almanac; call number; copyright date;** INTRODUCE **unabridged dictionary; thesaurus; verso**
3. REVIEW LMC Rules
4. REVIEW Local Circulation Procedures/Check Out Books
5. REVIEW Book Care Rules

Literature Appreciation
1. Fiction
   01. Types: Historical, Realistic; Humorous; Adventure
   02. Elements: Character; Plot; Setting
2. Nonfiction
   01. Folklore (Fables, Folktales, Fairy Tales)
   02. Poetry
   03. Biography
   04. Informational
3. Multicultural Literature
4. Authors/Illustrators
5. Award Books (Newbery; Coretta Scott King)

Information Skills
1. Location of Materials: REVIEW / EXTEND Arrangement of Fiction Books; Arrangement of Nonfiction Books & Arrangement of Biography Books; INTRODUCE Arrangement of Audiovisual Materials
2. Parts of a Book: REVIEW **table of contents; title page; glossary, index;** INTRODUCE **dedication**
3. Research: REVIEW/EXTEND Alphabetical Order; Use of the Encyclopedia; Use of the Dictionary; Use of Periodicals; Use of Special Reference Books ; INTRODUCE Use of Atlas; Use of Almanac; Children's Magazine Guide
4. Card/Computer Catalog: REVIEW /EXTEND Types of Cards/Searches & Card/Record Information

Technology
1. REVIEW/INTRODUCE Proper Use & Care of Appropriate AV Equipment & Software
2. REVIEW/INTRODUCE Viewing & Listening Skills

CURRICULUM CORRELATION

_____

_____

_____

_____

MATERIALS:
Book, Place My Words Are Looking For by Paul Janeczko
Transparency "Composing Cinquains" (see next page)
Overhead Projector and Transparency Pens
Paper and Pencils

FOCUS:
Define *poetry*. Give and elicit very general responses. Remind students that all poems do not need to rhyme and all aren't read with the same rhythm. Have a student find the word *poetry* in the dictionary for clarification and explain that poetry is usually an *emotional reaction* to something in everyday life. ***Tell the students that we're going to look at a book of poetry and then try our hands at some poetry, too.***

ACTIVITY:
Introduce the book Place My Words Are Looking For. Tell the students that several authors of poetry and books share their feelings about poetry. Read the interview with Cynthia Rylant.

Tell the students that we're going to write some poetry, but we're going to use a special form of poetry called *cinquain.* Point out that these poems have five lines. Tell students that the word *cinquain* comes from the Spanish word *cinco*, meaning *five.* Define cinquain as a verse about one subject. Each of the five lines gives particular information and must contain a certain number of syllables.

Show the transparency of cinquain form. Using the form, have the students write a cinquain as a class. Try to get suggestions from everyone. Brainstorm for answers and work on getting them into the correct form.

Read the class cinquain aloud. Be sure to read with expression since the poem is an expression about one's feelings about an object.

Example:

Tiger
Wild Meat-eater
Creeping, Growling, Snapping
And I Am Happy, But Afraid
Wild Cat

Erase the transparency, but leave the projector on so the students can see the form. Pass out paper and pencils and allow students to work on individual cinquains.

CLOSURE:
Have the students read their poems aloud, if they wish to do so.

EXTENSION:
Remind students that poetry books are located in the 800 section of the Dewey Decimal System. Have a student locate that section in the Library Media Center. Suggest other poetry books that the students may enjoy.

NOTES:
If you have access to word processing and graphics computer programs, such as The Print Shop by Brøderbund, have the students type their poems on the computer. If graphics are not available, have the students draw pictures to illustrate their poems. Display the finished products on the bulletin board.

PRACTICING POETRY
COMPOSING CINQUAINS

_____

Name an object - 2 syllables

_____

What is it like? - 4 syllables

_____

What does it do? - 6 syllables

_____

How does it make you feel? - 8 syllables

_____

What is another name for it? - 2 syllables

GRADE 4	LIBRARY MEDIA INSTRUCTIONAL PLAN	DATE_____

Dual Independence

LMC LEARNER STANDARDS

Orientation & Circulation
1. LMC Areas: REVIEW **Circulation Area; Fiction/Easy Section(s); Periodical Section; Reference Section; Nonfiction Section; Biography Section; Card/Computer Catalog**
2. Vocabulary: REVIEW **media; reference; fiction; nonfiction; periodicals; publisher; biography; atlas; almanac; call number; copyright date;** INTRODUCE **unabridged dictionary; thesaurus; verso**
3. REVIEW LMC Rules
4. REVIEW Local Circulation Procedures/Check Out Books
5. REVIEW Book Care Rules

Literature Appreciation
1. Fiction
   01. Types: Historical, Realistic; Humorous; Adventure
   02. Elements: Character; Plot; Setting
2. Nonfiction
   01. Folklore (Fables, Folktales, Fairy Tales)
   02. Poetry
   03. Biography
   04. Informational
3. Multicultural Literature
4. Authors/Illustrators
5. Award Books (Newbery; Coretta Scott King)

Information Skills
1. Location of Materials: REVIEW / EXTEND Arrangement of Fiction Books; Arrangement of Nonfiction Books & Arrangement of Biography Books; INTRODUCE Arrangement of Audiovisual Materials
2. Parts of a Book: REVIEW **table of contents; title page; glossary, index;** INTRODUCE **dedication**
3. Research: REVIEW/EXTEND Alphabetical Order; Use of the Encyclopedia; Use of the Dictionary; Use of Periodicals; Use of Special Reference Books ; INTRODUCE Use of Atlas; Use of Almanac; Children's Magazine Guide
4. Card/Computer Catalog: REVIEW /EXTEND Types of Cards/Searches & Card/Record Information

Technology
1. REVIEW/INTRODUCE Proper Use & Care of Appropriate AV Equipment & Software
2. REVIEW/INTRODUCE Viewing & Listening Skills

CURRICULUM CORRELATION

Social Studies

_____

_____

_____

MATERIALS:
Book, Fiesta by June Behrens; Map of North America
Word Cards: *WHO, WHAT, WHEN, WHERE, & WHY*
Overhead Projector, Blank Transparency Film, Transparency Pens
Encyclopedias & Nonfiction Books about Mexico; Pencils & Paper
Extension Project: Drawing Paper, Crayons

FOCUS:
Show the map of North America. Point out that Mexico is a part of North America, the same continent of which the U.S. is a part. Ask if any of the students have ever visited Mexico. If some have, let them share their memories. Ask what language is spoken in Mexico. Explain that the history of the United States is intertwined with that of Mexico because part of the U.S. once belonged to the country of Mexico, just like parts of the U.S. belonged to Spain, England and France. Explain that many Americans are of Hispanic descent because their ancestors came from Spain or Latin America, including Mexico. Point out that Mexico once belonged to Spain and France also. Ask the students to recall the date celebrated as Independence Day in the United States. Explain that Mexico has two Independence Days. *Tell the students that today we will look at these two special occasions celebrated by Hispanic people in Mexico and the United States.*

ACTIVITY:
Ask the students to describe a *fiesta* . Explain that people in Mexico love fiestas and celebrate many of their holidays with them. Share the book Fiesta with the students. Read the note at the end of the book.   Show the students the photograph on page eleven. Explain that the drawing of the man in the photograph is of Ignacio Zaragoza, the hero of the Battle of Puebla.

Divide the students into five groups, Give each group a word card and instruct the students to recall the information just presented about Cinco de Mayo. Start with the *WHAT* card. Have the students identify what happened in Mexican history to prompt this holiday (the Battle of Puebla). Next have the group identify *WHEN* the battle took place (May 5, 1862). The *WHERE* group can identify the location of the battle (the town of Puebla, Mexico). The *WHO* group can identify the hero of the battle (Ignacio Zaragoza) and the *WHY* group can identify the reason for the battle (to drive the French government out of Mexico).   Then write a paragraph on the overhead transparency identifying Cinco de Mayo. (On May 5, 1862, Ignacio Zaragoza led the Mexican troops in the battle of Puebla, in Puebla, Mexico. The Mexicans defeated the French soldiers, freeing Mexico from the French Government. Today Cinco de Mayo is celebrated as an Independence Day in Mexico.)

Remind the students that we're looking at two Mexican holidays. Distribute the books and encyclopedias and tell each group to find out the same information about the holiday, Diez y Seis de Septiembre. Give them the clue that *Septiembre* is the Spanish word for *September* so they are looking for an Independence Day that is celebrated in September. Walk around and work with each group. When the *WHEN* group has found the date of the holiday, have them find out the year that Mexico actually won it's independence from Spain. After each group has found the information, work as a class and write a paragraph about Diez y Seis de Septiembre. (On September 15, 1810, in Delores, Mexico, Father Hildago issued a proclamation that Mexico should fight for freedom from Spain. The actual freedom did not come until 1820. In Mexico, September 16th is celebrated as an Independence Day.)

CLOSURE:
Have the students make statements about the two Mexican Independence Days.

EXTENSION:
Have the students draw pictures of the events that take place during a Mexican fiesta.

NOTES:

GRADE 5	**LIBRARY MEDIA INSTRUCTIONAL PLAN**	**DATE**_____

Beanstalk Sprouts

LMC LEARNER STANDARDS
Orientation & Circulation
1. LMC Areas: REVIEW **Circulation Area; Fiction/Easy Section(s); Periodical Section; Reference Section; Nonfiction Section; Biography Section; Card/Computer Catalog**
2. Vocabulary: REVIEW **media; reference; fiction; nonfiction; periodicals; publisher; biography; atlas; almanac; INTRODUCE audio; visual; classics**
3. REVIEW LMC Rules
4. REVIEW Local Circulation Procedures/ Check Out Books
5. REVIEW Book Care Rules

Literature Appreciation
1. Fiction
  01. Types: Science Fiction; Historical; Realistic
  02. Character; Plot; Setting; Theme
2. Nonfiction
  01. Folklore (Fables, Folktales, Fairy Tales, Tall Tales)
  02. Poetry
  03. Biography
  04. Informational
3. Multicultural Literature
4. Award Books (Newbery; Wilder)
5. Authors/Illustrators

Information Skills
1. Location of Materials: REVIEW/EXTEND Arrangement of Fiction Books; Arrangement of Nonfiction Books; Arrangement of Biography Books; Arrangement of AV Materials
2. Parts of a Book: INTRODUCE **preface & copyright page**
3. Research: REVIEW /EXTEND Use of Encyclopedia; Use of Dictionary; Use of Periodicals; Use of Special Reference Books; Use of Atlas; Use of Almanac; Children's Magazine Guide; INTRODUCE Use of Thesaurus
4. Card/Computer Catalog: REVIEW/EXTEND Types of Cards/Searches & Card/Record Information
5. Dewey Decimal System: INTRODUCE Ten Classes

Technology
1. REVIEW/INTRODUCE Proper Use & Care of Appropriate AV Equipment
2. REVIEW/INTRODUCE Viewing & Listening Skills

CURRICULUM CORRELATION
_____

_____

_____

_____

_____

MATERIALS:
Book, Jack and the Beanstalk by Steven Kellogg
Beanstalk (Green line drawn on wide paper about 8 feet long)
Ten Green "Leaves" and a Black Marker
Extension Project:
Pencil, Paper, Glue and Green Crayon

FOCUS:

Have the students recall the meaning and origin of *Folklore*. Find England on a map or in an atlas. Tell them they'll hear a very familiar English fairy tale Jack and the Beanstalk. (Find out how many students knew that it is from England.) Explain that Jack had many decisions to make. Have the students listen carefully to identify all the decision points in the story. *Explain that after the story, we'll review the decision points to see if the outcome might have changed had Jack made some different, but not necessarily better, decisions.*

ACTIVITY:

Introduce the author/illustrator, Steven Kellogg. Tell the students that they have probably read other books written and illustrated by Steven Kellogg. Ask them to recall some of them. Read the book Jack and the Beanstalk.

Roll out the empty beanstalk. Review the sequence of the story, listing the following points where Jack had to make a decision. Answers will vary. As the students give the answers, write each one on a *leaf* and attach each decision leaf to the beanstalk, from the bottom up. Briefly discuss the various decisions Jack could have made.
•A stranger offers to buy Jack's cow for some *magic* beans. Should he sell the cow or not?
•Jack's Mom throws away the beans. Should he gather them up or leave them?
•Beans sprout and a giant beanstalk grows. Should he climb the beanstalk or not?
•Jack finds the Land of the Giants in the sky. Should he explore it or go back home?
•Jack sees the hen that lays golden eggs. Should he steal it or get out of there?
•Later Jack wants to go back for more treasure. Should he climb up the beanstalk again or be happy with his hen?
•Jack climbs the beanstalk and sees the Giant counting his gold. Should he steal it or not?
•Much later, Jack wants to go back up the beanstalk. Should he let well enough alone or go back for more?
•Jack sees the magic harp. Should he steal it or go back home?
•The Giant is after Jack. Should he chop down the beanstalk or run?

CLOSURE:

Remind the students that one characteristic of folktales is that they were originally spoken rather than written. Because of this, there are many versions of the story that vary slightly. Ask students to share any variations they may have heard. Remind the students that folktales are part of the Nonfiction Section of the LMC. They're found on the 300 shelves.

EXTENSION:

Divide the students into groups of three or four. Have each group select one leaf on the beanstalk where Jack could have made a different decision. Draw a branch at that point and have each group work together to come up with the new ending to explain how the story would have progressed if a different decision had been made at that point. Have them write a brief description of their *ending*. Attach it to the beanstalk where you have drawn the *branch*.

NOTES:

GRADE 5	LIBRARY MEDIA INSTRUCTIONAL PLAN	DATE_____

Big Dipper

LMC LEARNER STANDARDS
Orientation & Circulation
1. LMC Areas: REVIEW **Circulation Area; Fiction/Easy Section(s); Periodical Section; Nonfiction Section; Biography Section Reference Section; Card/Computer Catalog**
2. Vocabulary: REVIEW **media; reference; fiction; nonfiction; periodicals; publisher; biography; atlas; almanac;** INTRODUCE **audio; visual; classics**
3. REVIEW LMC Rules
4. REVIEW Local Circulation Procedures/ Check Out Books
5. REVIEW Book Care Rules

Literature Appreciation
1. Fiction
   01. Types: Science Fiction; Historical; Realistic
   02. Character; Plot; Setting; Theme
2. Nonfiction
   01. Folklore (Fables, Folktales, Fairy Tales; Tall Tales)
   02. Poetry
   03. Biography
   04. Informational
3. Multicultural Literature
4. Award Books (Newbery; Wilder)
5. Authors/Illustrators

Information Skills
1. Location of Materials: REVIEW/EXTEND Arrangement of Fiction Books; Arrangement of Nonfiction Books; Arrangement of Biography Books; Arrangement of AV Materials
2. Parts of a Book: INTRODUCE **preface & copyright page**
3. Research: REVIEW /EXTEND Use of Encyclopedia; Use of Dictionary; Use of Periodicals; Use of Special Reference Books; Use of Atlas; Use of Almanac; Children's Magazine Guide; INTRODUCE Use of Thesaurus
4. Card/Computer Catalog: REVIEW/EXTEND Types of Cards/Searches & Card/Record Information
5. Dewey Decimal System: INTRODUCE Ten Classes

Technology
1. REVIEW/INTRODUCE Proper Use & Care of Appropriate AV Equipment
2. REVIEW/INTRODUCE Viewing & Listening Skills

CURRICULUM CORRELATION
Social Studies
_____
Science
_____
_____
_____
_____

MATERIALS:
Videotape, Follow the Drinking Gourd (American School Publishers), VCR, TV
Book, Follow the Drinking Gourd by Jeanette Winter
Book, Picture Life of Harriet Tubman by David Adler
Map of the United States
Projection of the Big Dipper (Using a flashlight with a large lens, cut a circle from black posterboard the same size as the lens. Punch small holes in the posterboard to represent the stars in the Big Dipper. Punch a slightly larger hole for the North Star. Place the circle over the lens of the flashlight and use electrical tape to seal the edges.)
Extension Project:
Book, The Drinking Gourd by F. N. Monjo

FOCUS:
Ask the students if they ever sit outside at night and just look at the stars. Ask them if they've noticed that the stars create certain shapes like the Big Dipper and the Little Dipper. Show the projection of the Big Dipper. Discuss the shape of the Big Dipper and why it has that name. Point out that the directly above the front edge of the Big Dipper is the North Star. Point out that in the past there were other names for this star constellation. *Tell the students that we're going to look back in history to the days just before the Civil War in the United States, when a few lucky slaves were led to freedom by a group of people who believed in freedom, and we'll see how the stars were important in these escapes.* Discuss the vocabulary: *Civil War; slavery; plantation; abolitionist; Underground Railroad; drinking gourd; conductor; constellation; Big Dipper.* Ask the students what was happening in America at the time. Briefly discuss the issues: the North was an industrial area and the South was agricultural area. Most of the slaves lived in the South and worked on the farms and plantations. Many slaves ran away and tried to go somewhere where they could be free. Often they went to Canada.

ACTIVITY:
Show the map of the United States and point out the southern states. Ask the students to find Canada and decide the direction that the slaves would travel to get there. Explain that most slaves could not read, so even if they could get a map, they wouldn't be able to use it to find Canada. Tell the students that they used the stars as their guide, just as sailors did on long voyages across the sea. Explain also that they had to use songs and secret signs to communicate this information to each other.

Show the video. Explain that although it is a fictionalized story, it is based on historical fact. Read the words of the song from the book. Discuss how the song was a secret message to slaves that could guide them to freedom.

Ask the students to identify Harriet Tubman. Explain that she was one of the most successful *conductors* on the *Underground Railroad.* Read the biography or parts to the biography about Harriet Tubman.

CLOSURE:
Discuss why the slaves wanted to be free and why people like Harriet Tubman wanted to help them. Discuss the dangers they might face on their journey.

EXTENSION:
The book The Drinking Gourd offers the same kind of story as Follow the Drinking Gourd, but from the viewpoint of the white abolitionists who also helped slaves escape to freedom. Read this book and have the students decide what they would have done in the same situation.

NOTES:

GRADE 5	LIBRARY MEDIA INSTRUCTIONAL PLAN	DATE_____

Plot Against a President

LMC LEARNER STANDARDS

Orientation & Circulation
1. LMC Areas: REVIEW **Circulation Area;**
   Fiction/Easy Section(s); Periodical Section;
   Nonfiction Section; Biography Section
   Reference Section; Card/Computer Catalog
2. Vocabulary: REVIEW **media; reference;**
   fiction; nonfiction; periodicals; publisher;
   biography; atlas; almanac; INTRODUCE
   audio; visual; classics
3. REVIEW LMC Rules
4. REVIEW Local Circulation Procedures/
   Check Out Books
5. REVIEW Book Care Rules

Literature Appreciation
1. Fiction
   01. Types: Science Fiction; Historical;
   Realistic
   02. Character; Plot; Setting; Theme
2. Nonfiction
   01. Folklore (Fables, Folktales, Fairy Tales;
   Tall Tales)
   02. Poetry
   03. Biography
   04. Informational
3. Multicultural Literature
4. Award Books (Newbery; Wilder)
5. Authors/Illustrators

Information Skills
1. Location of Materials: REVIEW/EXTEND
   Arrangement of Fiction Books; Arrangement
   of Nonfiction Books; Arrangement of
   Biography Books; Arrangement of AV
   Materials
2. Parts of a Book: INTRODUCE **preface &**
   copyright page
3. Research: REVIEW /EXTEND
   Use of Encyclopedia; Use of Dictionary; Use
   of Periodicals; Use of Special Reference
   Books; Use of Atlas; Use of Almanac;
   Children's Magazine Guide; INTRODUCE
   Use of Thesaurus
4. Card/Computer Catalog: REVIEW/EXTEND
   Types of Cards/Searches & Card/Record
   Information
5. Dewey Decimal System: INTRODUCE Ten
   Classes

Technology
1. REVIEW/INTRODUCE Proper Use & Care
   of Appropriate AV Equipment
2. REVIEW/INTRODUCE Viewing &
   Listening Skills

CURRICULUM CORRELATION
Social Studies

_____

_____

_____

_____

_____

MATERIALS:

Book, Detective Pinkerton and Mr. Lincoln by William Wise
Map of the United States
Activity Sheet "Abraham Lincoln Acrostic" (see next page)
Access to an Atlas, Almanac, Dictionary, Card/Computer Catalog, and Encyclopedia

FOCUS:

Have the students recall the name of the war which took place in the U.S. between the years 1860 and 1865. Ask why the Civil War was fought. Point out the differences in the lifestyles of the citizens living in the North and South. Explain that slavery had been an issue for many years, but the war did not actually begin until South Carolina seceded from the Union. Discuss the following vocabulary words: *secession; abolitionists; treason; detective; investigation.* Find the following locations on the map: *Chicago, Philadelphia, Baltimore, New York, Washington, D.C., Wilmington, Harve de Grace, New York,* and *Susquehanna River.* ***Tell the students that we're going to find out about a little-known event in the life of a well-known President of the United States, Abraham Lincoln.***

ACTIVITY:

Have the students recall facts that they already know about Abraham Lincoln. Introduce the book and read to the top of page 21, including the "Note to the Reader" at the very beginning.

Stop reading before you tell the students about the important event which was about to take place.

Distribute the Activity Sheets and have the students answer each of the thirteen questions. The students will already know some of the answers. Other questions will need to be researched by the students. If they don't know an answer, discuss where the students could find the answers. Let a few students find each answer. When all the answers have been found and written in the blanks, complete the question at the bottom of the page. The answers to the questions are:

     1. Beezus; 2. Italy; 3. Fudge; 4. Newbery; 5. Nebraska; 6. Nonfiction;
     7. Biography; 8. Hot; 9. Wilder; 10. Mary; 11. Science; 12. Sounder;
     13. Tad

The answer to the puzzle is: *The plotters were planning to assassinate Abraham Lincoln.* Discuss the meaning of *assassinate.*

Read the next three paragraphs in the book. Discuss with the students that the assassination attempt was obviously thwarted because the year of this event was 1860 and John Wilkes Booth killed Lincoln in 1865.

CLOSURE:

Discuss with the students how history might have been changed if Abraham Lincoln had been assassinated before the Civil War. He was a powerful president and was a symbol of strength for the North. Have the students speculate how their lives would be different if the South had won the war. We can, however, conclude that slavery would have disappeared before now just as it has the world over. We might be an agricultural country instead of an industrial one. There might be two separate countries.

EXTENSION:

Ask the classroom teacher to read the rest of book in the classroom.

NOTES:

The book Detective Pinkerton and Mr. Lincoln is out of print, but many copies are available at secondary sources. Try a used book store or borrow the book from the local public library. The Activity Sheet can also be made into a transparency and completed as a class.

Name _____   Class _____

Detective Pinkerton and Mr. Lincoln Acrostic

Directions: Using the card catalog, reference books or even the books on the shelves of the Library Media Center, answer the questions below by writing the answers in the blanks to the right. When you have completed all the **clue words**, arrange the letters within the rectangle by their numbers and put them in order below to discover what the rebels were plotting in 1860 in the city of Baltimore, Maryland.

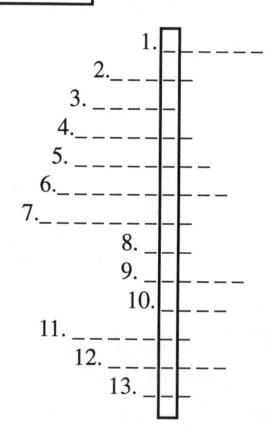

1. In the *Ramona* books by Beverly Cleary, Ramona had a nickname for her sister, Beatrice. What was it?

2. This country in Europe is shaped like a boot.

3. In the book, Tales of a Fourth Grade Nothing, What is the nickname of Peter's little brother?

4. What award did Russell Freeman win for his book Lincoln: a Photobiography?

5. Lincoln is the capital city of what state?

6. What kind of books are arranged by their Dewey Decimal numbers?

7. What is a book about a person's life called?

8. What is the definition of the word *sweltering*?

9. What is the last name of the author of the *Little House* books?

10. What was the first name of President Lincoln's widow?

11. What kind of books are found in the 500 section of the nonfiction books.

12. What book by William Armstrong is about a boy and his dog?

13. What was the name of Lincoln's youngest son?

The plotters in Baltimore were planning to:

_ _ _ _ _ _ _ _ _ _ _   _ _ _ _ _ _ _   _ _ _ _ _ _
13 5 5 13 5 5 9 12 13 6 3   13 1 4 13 7 13 10   2 9 12 11 8 2 12

| GRADE 6 | LIBRARY MEDIA INSTRUCTIONAL PLAN | DATE_____ |

A Car's Life

LMC LEARNER STANDARDS

Orientation & Circulation
1. LMC Areas: REVIEW **Circulation Area;
   Fiction/Easy Section(s); Periodical Section;
   Reference Section; Nonfiction Section;
   Biography Section;** Card/Computer Catalog
2. Vocabulary REVIEW **media; fiction;
   reference; nonfiction; periodicals; publisher;
   biography; atlas; audio; visual; classics;**
   INTRODUCE **autobiography**
3. REVIEW LMC Rules
4. REVIEW Local Circulation Procedures/ Check
   Out Books
5. REVIEW Book Care Rules

Literature Appreciation
1. Fiction
   01. All Types
   02. Character; Plot; Setting; Theme; Style
2. Nonfiction
   01. Folklore (Fables, Folktales, Fairy Tales;
   Tall Tales; Mythology & Legends)
   02. Poetry
   03. Biography/Autobiography
3. Multicultural Literature
4. Award Books (Newbery; Carnegie; Coretta
   Scott King)
5. Authors/Illustrators

Information Skills
1. Location of Materials: REVIEW/EXTEND
   Arrangement of Fiction Books; Arrangement of
   Nonfiction Books; Arrangement of Biography
   Books & Arrangement of AV Materials
2. Parts of a Book: REVIEW **preface; copyright
   page;** INTRODUCE **bibliography; footnotes;
   preface; appendices**
3. Research: REVIEW/EXTEND Use of
   Encyclopedia; Use of Periodicals; Use of
   Special Reference Books; Use of Atlas; Use
   of Almanac; Use of Thesaurus; Children's
   Magazine Guide; REINFORCE Outlining for
   Research
4. Card/Computer Catalog: REVIEW/EXTEND
   Types of Card/Searches & Card/Record
   Information
5. Dewey Decimal System: REVIEW/EXTEND
   Ten Classes & Recognize Subject of Each

Technology
1. REVIEW/INTRODUCE Proper Uses & Care
   of Appropriate Audiovisual Equipment
2. REVIEW/INTRODUCE Viewing &
   Listening Skills

CURRICULUM CORRELATION
Social Studies
_____
_____
_____
_____

MATERIALS:
Several Biography Books by Jean Fritz, Including <u>Homecoming, My Own Story</u>
Filmstrip, <u>Homecoming, My Own Story</u> (American School Publishers); Filmstrip
    Projector
Chalk and Chalkboard , or Vocabulary Board
Vocabulary Cards of the Vocabulary Words
Extension Project: Markers and a Ruler or Yardstick
<u>Timeliner</u> Computer Program, Computer and Printer or a Long Roll of Paper

FOCUS:
Have students define *biography* as a book about a person's life. Ask them if they know
the meaning of the word *autobiography*. (It is *not* the story of a car's life!) Write
autobiography on the chalkboard or find it on the vocabulary board. Look at its parts
- *auto* - *bio* - *graphy*. Explain that *bio* is the Greek word for *life* and *graph* comes from
the Greek word, *graphon* which means *written*, so that a biography is a written account
of a person's life. Try to derive the meaning of *auto* as *self*, using other words that
begin with *auto* like *automatic, automobile* and *autograph*. Define *autobiography* as
a book about a person's life written by that person. ***Explain to the students that we'll
look at a fictionalized autobiography and discover an author who is famous for the
biographies she's written.***

ACTIVITY:
Explain that we will discover an author who has become famous for writing
biographies of people in American history. Introduce the author Jean Fritz to the
students. Show them some of the many books she has written. Tell the students that
in 1986, Jean Fritz was awarded the Laura Ingalls Wilder Award, which is given only
once every five years by the American Library Association to an author who has
written many books for children, and whose books will remain interesting to students
for many years.

Explain that Jean Fritz was fascinated with American history because she did not live
in America as a child. Her father worked for the YMCA and they lived in China until
Jean was twelve years old. Point out that she wrote the book about her life in China
and show the class the book <u>Homecoming</u>. Explain that because she wrote the book
as a story, it is not classified as *autobiography,* but as *fiction* and is called *fictionalized
autobiography.* You may want to read the author's *forward* in the front of the book.
Find the country of China and the Yangtze River on a map or in an atlas.

Discuss the vocabulary words: *revolution, bund, aman, coolie, bound feet,* and
foreign devil. Show the filmstrip.

CLOSURE:
Tell the students that Jean Fritz won the Newbery Honor Medal for this book. Review
the meaning of the Newbery Medal. Review the vocabulary words to find out if the
students found the words in the filmstrip and answer any questions the students may
have about the filmstrip. Review the definitions of *biography, autobiography* and
fictionalized autobiography. The students may be familiar with the *Little House*
books by Laura Ingalls Wilder, which are also a kind of *fictionalized biography*.

EXTENSION:
As a class, make a timeline of the important events in the life of Jean Fritz. The
timeline can be printed using the computer program <u>Timeliner</u> by Tom Snyder
Productions, if available.

NOTES:
This lesson may last two or even three class sessions in the LMC and can be done in
conjunction with a classroom assignment on biographies.

GRADE 6	LIBRARY MEDIA INSTRUCTIONAL PLAN	DATE_____

Cinderella Tales

LMC LEARNER STANDARDS
Orientation & Circulation
1. LMC Areas: REVIEW **Circulation Area; Fiction/Easy Section(s); Periodical Section; Reference Section; Nonfiction Section; Biography Section; Card/Computer Catalog**
2. Vocabulary REVIEW **media; fiction; reference; nonfiction; periodicals; publisher; biography; atlas; audio; visual; classics;** INTRODUCE **autobiography**
3. REVIEW LMC Rules
4. REVIEW Local Circulation Procedures/ Check Out Books
5. REVIEW Book Care Rules

Literature Appreciation
1. Fiction
  01. All Types
  02. Character; Plot; Setting; Theme; Style
2. Nonfiction
  01. Folklore (Fables, Folktales, Fairy Tales, Tall Tales; Mythology & Legends)
  02. Poetry
  03. Biography/Autobiography
3. Multicultural Literature
4. Award Books (Newbery; Carnegie; Coretta Scott King)
5. Authors/Illustrators

Information Skills
1. Location of Materials: REVIEW/EXTEND Arrangement of Fiction Books; Arrangement of Nonfiction Books; Arrangement of Biography Books & Arrangement of AV Materials
2. Parts of a Book: REVIEW **preface; copyright page;** INTRODUCE **bibliography; footnotes; preface; appendices**
3. Research: REVIEW/EXTEND Use of Encyclopedia; Use of Periodicals; Use of Special Reference Books; Use of Atlas ; Use of Almanac; Use of Thesaurus; Children's Magazine Guide; REINFORCE Outlining for Research
4. Card/Computer Catalog: REVIEW/EXTEND Types of Cards/Searches & Card/Record Information
5. Dewey Decimal System: REVIEW/EXTEND Ten Classes & Recognize Subject of Each

Technology
1. REVIEW/INTRODUCE Proper Use & Care of Appropriate Audiovisual Equipment
2. REVIEW/INTRODUCE Viewing & Listening Skills

CURRICULUM CORRELATION
Social Studies

_____

_____

_____

MATERIALS:
Books: Talking Eggs by Robert San Souci (Louisiana)
    Egyptian Cinderella by Shirley Climo (Egypt)
    Yeh-Shen by Ai-Ling Louie (China)
    Mufaro's Beautiful Daughters by John Steptoe (Africa)
Cinderella Folktale Chart (see next page)
Pencils and Paper

FOCUS:
In early times, when most people could not write, stories were spoken rather than written. There were stories told in almost every culture with similar themes and characters. This was the beginning of folk literature. *Tell the students that we will analyze several folktales from different cultures to find the similar story elements.*

ACTIVITY:
Brainstorm with the students to have them recall the story of Cinderella. If necessary, read them one of the many versions.

Reproduce the chart (blank, with no answers filled in) on large poster board before the lesson. Introduce the chart to the students and explain the meaning of each of the story elements.

Have the students respond verbally to identify the story elements of Cinderella as you write an answer in each box on the chart.

Explain that, while the story of Cinderella that we are most familiar with is based on a story written in France by Charles Perrault, other cultures have similar stories about a poor mistreated girl who is helped by a magical assistant to overcome her greedy rivals and live happily ever after.

Introduce the four books listed above as *Cinderella* stories from other cultures. Identify the origin of each story. Introduce any unfamiliar vocabulary in each of the books.

CLOSURE:
Divide the students into four groups and assign each group one of the books to discuss among themselves. After the group discussion, one member of each group will retell the story to the class. As each story is finished, complete the chart. Answers will vary. Have the students study the chart and discuss the similarities and differences among the various stories.

EXTENSION:
Explain that we can create some original modern folktales set in our own time with events and problems faced by kids today. Have the class brainstorm each of the story elements on the chart. Complete the information for each box, except the title. Have each student create a title and write an original contemporary story based on the story elements the class has created.

NOTES:
The students should already have some background knowledge of the origin of folktales. This lesson could be extended to create a unit on Folk Literature. Even as one lesson, it will probably take two or three class sessions to complete.

ELEMENTS OF A FOLKTALE - CINDERELLA

Title & Author	Setting	Time Period	Main Charactors — Heroine	Main Charactors — Villains	Magical Helper	Point of Conflict	Proof of Identity	Fate of Villains	Happy Ending
Cinderella by Charles Perrault	France	Medieval Times of Kings and Castles	Cinderella	Step-mother and Step-sisters	Fairy Godmother	The "Ball" at the Palace	Glass Slipper	They Were Forgiven	Cinderella and the Prince Were Married
Talking Eggs by Robert San Souci	Louisiana	Late 1800s	Blanche	Mother and Rose (sister)	Old Woman	Blanche Returns with Jewels and a Carriage	Charity and Obedience	They're Left in the Woods Looking for the Old Woman	Blanche Moves to the City & Lives as a Grand Lady
Egyptian Cinderella by Shirley Climo	Egypt	Ancient History	Rhodopis	Household Servant Girls	Horus, the Falcon	The Pharoah Holds Court for His Subjects	Rose-Red Slipper	They Remain as Servants	She Marries the Pharoah & Becomes the Queen of Egypt
Yeh Shen by Ai-Ling Louise	China	Ancient History 222 BC	Yeh-Shen	Step-mother and Step-sister	Magical Fish	There is a Festival in the Spring	Golden Slippers	They Die in a Shower of Falling Rocks	Yeh-Shen Marries the King and Becomes the Queen
Mufaro's Beautiful Daughters by John Steptoe	Africa	Long Ago	Nyasha	Manyara, Her Sister	Snake	The King is Looking for a Wife	Kindness and Unselfishness	Manyara Becomes a Servant for Her Sister	Nyasha Marries the King and Becomes the Queen
Sample Story Elements for Original Folktale	USA	Modern Times	Carla	Jennifer, a girl in Carla's Class	Magical Coin	There is a Contest and the Prize is a Trip to Hawaii	Honesty	Jennifer and Her Family Move to Another State	Carla Wins the Contest and Goes to Hawaii

GRADE 6	LIBRARY MEDIA INSTRUCTIONAL PLAN	DATE_____

Coretta Scott King Award

LMC LEARNER STANDARDS

Orientation & Circulation
1. LMC Location: REVIEW **Circulation Area; Fiction/Easy Section(s); Periodical Section; Reference Section; Nonfiction Section; Biography Section; Card/Computer Catalog**
2. Vocabulary REVIEW **media; fiction; reference; nonfiction; periodicals; publisher; biography; atlas; audio; visual; classics;** INTRODUCE **autobiography**
3. REVIEW LMC Rules
4. REVIEW Local Circulation Procedures/ Check Out Books
5. REVIEW Book Care Rules

Literature Appreciation
1. Fiction
   01. All Types
   02. Character; Plot; Setting; Theme; Style
2. Nonfiction
   01. Folklore (Fables, Folktales, Fairy Tales; Tall Tales; Mythology & Legends)
   02. Poetry
   03. Biography/Autobiography
   3. Multicultural Literature
   4. Award Books (Newbery; Coretta Scott King; Carnegie)
   5. Authors/Illustrators

Information Skills
1. Location of Materials: REVIEW/EXTEND Arrangement of Fiction Books; Arrangement of Nonfiction Books; Arrangement of Biography Books & Arrangement of AV Materials
2. Parts of a Book: REVIEW **preface; copyright page;** INTRODUCE **bibliography; footnotes; preface; appendices**
3. Research: REVIEW/EXTEND Use of Encyclopedia; Use of Periodicals; Use of Special Reference Books; Use of Atlas ; Use of Almanac; Use of Thesaurus; Children's Magazine Guide; REINFORCE Outlining for Research
4. Card/Computer Catalog: REVIEW/EXTEND Types of Cards/Searches & Card/Record Information
5. Dewey Decimal System: REVIEW/EXTEND Ten Classes & Recognize Subject of Each

Technology
1. REVIEW/INTRODUCE Proper Use & Care of Appropriate Audiovisual Equipment
2. REVIEW/INTRODUCE Viewing & Listening Skills

CURRICULUM CORRELATION

Social Studies

Art

_____

_____

_____

_____

MATERIALS:
Book, Coretta Scott King, a Woman of Peace by Paula Taylor
Bronze Coretta Scott King Award Seal
Drawing Paper and Pencils
Description of the Medal and List of Winners (see next page)
Extension Project: Book, Tar Beach by Faith Ringgold

FOCUS:
Have the students recall the name of the award given each year by the American Library Association to the illustrator of the book, published in America, with the most outstanding illustrations (Caldecott). Ask them to name the award given by the same group to the author of the most outstanding book written for young people and published in America (Newbery). *Tell the students that today we will look at another award presented by the American Library Association each year to an African American author and an African American illustrator.*

ACTIVITY:
Explain that this award is made in honor of the late Dr. Martin Luther King, Jr. Have the students recall any information that they know about him. Summarize that Martin Luther King, Jr. was a leader among African Americans that emphasized peaceful co-existence among people of all races and culture and that this change toward equal rights for all should be nonviolent.

Tell the students that the award is not named after Martin Luther King, Jr. It's named after his wife. Ask the students if they know her name. Show the students the biography book Coretta Scott King, a Woman of Peace. Read the short introductory note and have the students share any knowledge that they have about her.

Explain that the Coretta Scott King Award is given to both an African American author and an African American illustrator who have written or illustrated a book for young people that demonstrates the contributions of people of all cultures toward peace and harmony in the American way of life.

Tell the students that the winners of this award receive a medal just as the winners of the Caldecott and Newbery Awards do. Explain that before we look at the medal, they will have a chance to design medals which they think could represent this award. Discuss possible shapes for the medal and the significance of the shapes. (A circle might represent continuity, a triangle could stand for three concepts, such as peace, love and harmony. A star could represent reaching for new heights. A dove usually represents peace.) Discuss the pictures that could be represented on the medal such as Martin Luther King, Jr., Coretta Scott King, or a book.

Divide the students into groups of five or six. Distribute the paper and pencils and allow the students time to discuss and draw the medals. There will be only one drawing from each group. Have the groups share their completed drawings with the class.

CLOSURE:
Show the students the seal of the Coretta Scott King Medal. Tell them that Lev Mills is the artist who designed the medal and each part of the design has a meaning (see next page).

EXTENSION:
Read the book Tar Beach and have the students discuss why they think the illustrator of this book received the Coretta Scott King Medal.

NOTES:

Coretta Scott King Award

The Coretta Scott King Award was established in 1969 by a librarian, Glyndon Greer. The medal is awarded annually to African America authors and illustrators whose books demonstrate the effort to recognize the importance and significance of all cultures in the struggle for peace, harmony and equality among all people in America. The award was established in the memory of Martin Luther King, Jr. and was named to honor his wife who continues to work courageously to keep his dream alive. The first award, in 1970, was presented to an author and in 1974, a category was added for an illustrator. Since 1982, the Coretta Scott King Award has been officially affiliated with the American Library Association.

That same year the seal of the official medal was designed by Lev Mills in Atlanta, Georgia. Each part of the design has significance. The pyramid represents strength and the circle symbolizes continuous movement and change of ideas. The picture of the black child reading demonstrates that the award is given to a children's book. There are five religious symbols to show that Dr. Martin Luther King represented people of all religious beliefs, not just his own. The concepts of Peace and Brotherhood are connected from lines originating with the picture of the dove, which also symbolizes peace.

Recipients

1970 - <u>Dr. Martin Luther King, Jr., Man of Peace</u> by Lillie Patterson

1971 - <u>Black Troubadour: Langston Hughes</u> by Charlemae Rollins

1972 - <u>Seventeen Black Artists</u> by Elton Fax

1973 - <u>I Never Had It Made: the Autobiography of Jackie Robinson</u> by Alfred Duckett

1974 - <u>Ray Charles</u> by Sharon Bell Mathis (Author)
      <u>Ray Charles</u> illustrated by George Ford (Illustrator)

1975 - <u>The Legend of Africania</u> by Dorothy Robinson

1976 - <u>Duey's Tale</u> by Pearl Bailey

1977 - <u>The Story of Stevie Wonder</u> by James Haskins

1978 - <u>Africa Dream</u> by Eloise Greenfield

1979 - <u>Escape to Freedom</u> by Ossie Davis (Author)
      <u>Something on My Mind</u> by Nikki Grimes; illustrated by Tom Feelings (Illustrator)

1980 - <u>The Young Landlords</u> by Walter Dean Myers (Author)
      <u>Cornrows</u> by Camille Yarbrough; illustrated by Carole Byard (Illustrator)

1981 - <u>This Life</u> by Sidney Poitier (Author)
      <u>Beat the Story Drum</u> by Ashley Bryan (Illustrator)

1982 - <u>Let the Circle Be Unbroken</u> by Mildred Taylor (Author)
      <u>Mother Crocodile</u> translated by Rosa Guy; illustrated by John Steptoe (Illustrator)

1983 - <u>Sweet Whispers, Brother Rush</u> by Virginia Hamilton (Author)
      <u>Black Child</u> by Peter Magubane (Illustrator)

1984 - _Everett Anderson's Goodbye_ by Lucille Clifton (Author)

My Mama Needs Me by Mildred Pitts Walter; Illustrated by Pat Cummings (Illustrator)

1985 - _Motown and Didi_ by Walter Dean Myers (Author)

1986 - _The People Could Fly_ by Virginia Hamilton (Author)

The Patchwork Quilt by Valerie Flournoy; illustrated by Jerry Pinkney (Illustrator)

1987- _Justin and the Best Biscuits in the World_ by Mildred Pitts Walter (Author)

Half a Moon and One Whole Star by Crescent Dragonwagon; illustrated by Jerry Pinkney (Illustrator)

1988 - _The Friendship_ by Mildred Taylor (Author)

Mufaro's Beautiful Daughters by John Steptoe (Illustrator)

1989 - _Fallen Angels_ by Walter Dean Myers (Author)

Mirandy and Brother Wind by Patricia McKissack; illustrated by Jerry Pinkney (Illustrator)

1990 - _A Long Hard Journey_ by Patricia and Fredrick McKissack (Author)

Nathaniel Talking by Eloise Greenfield; illustrated by Jan Spivey Gilchrist (Illustrator)

1991 - _The Road to Memphis_ by Mildred Taylor (Author)

Aïda by Leontyne Price; illustrated by Leo and Diane Dillon (Illustrator)

1992 - _Now Is Your Time: the African American Struggle for Freedom_ by Walter Dean Myers (Author)

Tar Beach by Faith Ringgold (Illustrator)

1993 - _Dark Thirty_ by Patricia McKissack (Author)

Origin of Life on Earth retold by David Anderson; illustrated by Katherine Wilson (Illustrator)

RESOURCES

Ahlberg, Janet and Allan. *The Jolly Postman*. Boston: Little, Brown and Company, 1986. This *book* is actually a collection of letters that fairy tale characters might have sent to each other.

Behrens, June. *Fiesta!* Chicago: Children's Press, 1978. Using photographs and simple text, the author describes the celebration of the Mexican and Mexican-American holiday, Cinco de Mayo.

———. *Gung Hay Fat Chow*. Chicago: Children's Press, 1982. Using photographs and simple text, the author describes the celebration of Chinese New Year.

Burningham, John. *Mr. Gumpy's Outing*. New York: Henry Holt and Company, 1970. A congenial Englishman agrees to take some children and animals for a boat ride, which turns into disaster as Mr. Gumpy remains calm.

Carle, Eric. *The Very Hungry Caterpillar*. New York: Putnam, 1969. A caterpillar hatches from an egg and eats his way to a life as a beautiful butterfly.

Climo, Shirley. *The Egyptian Cinderella*. New York: Crowell, 1989. A slave girl held by the Egyptians becomes their queen in this *Cinderella* story.

D'Aulaire, Ingri and Edgar. *Abraham Lincoln*. New York: Doubleday, 1957. The authors present a picture book biography of the sixteenth U.S. president.

———. *Benjamin Franklin*. New York: Doubleday, 1950. A picture book story of this famous inventor and historical figure is presented in this now classic biography.

———. *Buffalo Bill*. New York: Doubleday, 1952. The authors travelled the West to collect information for a biography about this famous cowboy.

———. *Christopher Columbus*. New York: Doubleday, 1955. The authors present an interesting picture book biography of the famous explorer.

———. *George Washington*. New York: Doubleday, 1936. The authors present a picture book biography of the first U.S. president.

———. *Leif, the Lucky*. New York: Doubleday, 1951. The authors present a picture book biography of the Viking explorer, Leif Erickson.

———. *Pocahontas*. New York: Doubleday, 1949. The life of the famous Indian princess who aided the first English settlers in the New World is portrayed in this classic biography.

DePaola, Tomie. *The Cloud Book*. New York: Holiday House, 1975. The kinds of clouds and their functions are explained in a simple way with colorful illustrations.

Greenaway, Kate. *A Apple Pie*. London: Warne, n.d. The author uses the letters of the alphabet to describe all the things that children can do to get a piece of apple pie.

———. *Under the Window*. London, England : Warne, n.d. The well-known British author and illustrator illustrates her rhymes with pictures of pretty, happy eighteenth-century children in soft, pastel settings.

Hutchins, Pat. *The Wind Blew*. New York: Macmillan Publishing Company, 1974. Whipping through the English countryside, a gust of wind plays havoc with people and their belongings.

Janeczko, Paul. *Place My Words Are Looking For*. New York: Bradbury Press, 1990. Several well-known poets share their poems and their feelings about writing them.

Kaye, Marilyn. *The Real Tooth Fairy*. San Diego: Harcourt Brace Jovanovich, Inc., 1990. When a little girl loses her first tooth, she thinks her mother is the Tooth Fairy and is disappointed when a playmate at school thinks his dad is the Tooth Fairy.

Keeping, Charles. *Charley, Charlotte and the Golden Canary*. New York: Franklin Watts, 1967. Charley, a young boy growing up in London, is lonely when his best friend moves away so he earns money to buy a canary for companionship.

Kellogg, Steven. *Jack and the Beanstalk*. New York: William Morrow, and Company, 1991. The author/illustrator offers a colorful traditional version of the English fairy tale.

Lionni, Leo. *Alexander, and the Wind-up Mouse*. New York: Pantheon Books, 1969. Alexander, the mouse, discovers that the grass is not always greener on the other side of the fence.

————. *Frederick.* New York: Pantheon, 1967. A group of mice gather the things they'll need for the winter and one of them gathers something more important than food.

————. *Matthew's Dream.* New York: Alfred A. Knopf, 1991. A young mouse has higher aspirations than his family expects of him.

Louie, Ai-Ling. *Yeh-Shen.* New York: Philomel, 1982. The author retells a Chinese folk tale similar to the well-know fairy tale, *Cinderella.*

Martin, Bill, Jr. *Listen to the Rain.* New York: Henry Holt and Company, 1988. The author uses descriptive words and stylistic illustrations to describe a rainstorm from beginning to end.

Mayer, Mercer. *There's a Nightmare in My Closet.* New York: Dial, 1968. A little boy is afraid of the dark until he confronts the imaginary monster in his closet.

Monjo, F. N. *The Drinking Gourd.* New York: Harper, 1970. The author describes a fictionalized version of a family of slaves escaping to freedom on the Underground Railroad in America just before the Civil War.

Potter, Beatrix. *Animal Homes.* New York: Warne, 1991. Using brief text and illustrations from the original tales by Beatrix Potter, this board book shows several animals in their natural habitats.

————. *Dinner Time.* New York: Warne, 1991. Using brief text and illustrations from the original tales by Beatrix Potter, this board book shows the foods eaten by several animals.

————. *Farmyard Noises.* New York: Warne, 1991. Using brief text and illustrations from the original tales by Beatrix Potter, this board book introduces several farm animals and the sounds they make.

————. *Happy Families.* New York: Warne, 1991. Using brief text and illustrations from the original tales by Beatrix Potter, this board book shows several animal families and explains the terms used to describe their babies.

————. *Peter Rabbit: a Lift-the-Flap Rebus Book.* New York: Warne, 1991. The original story about the mischievous rabbit is presented in large clear type using pictures for some of the words.

Ringgold, Faith. *Tar Beach.* New York: Crown Publishers, 1991. A little girl dreams of flying above her home in Harlem and of giving all that she sees below her as a gift to her family.

Rowland, Della. *Little Red Riding Hood/The Wolf's Tale.* New York: Birch Lane Press, 1991. In this "Upside Down Tale," the reader hears the traditional tale and the story as told from the wolf's point of view.

Sabin, Louis. *Amazing World of Butterflies and Moths.* Mahwah: Troll Associates, 1982. Facts about the lives of butterflies and moths are presented.

Sadler, Marilyn. *Alistair in Outer Space.* New York: Simon and Schuster, 1984. Alistair, a very prompt child, is abducted by aliens from outer space and is afraid he'll be late in returning his books to the library.

San Souci, Robert. *The Talking Eggs.* New York: Dial Books, 1989. A *Cinderella* story from Louisiana in which the heroine, Rose, finds riches inside a basketful of eggs that talk to her.

Scieszka, Jon. *The True Story of the Three Little Pigs.* New York: Viking Press, 1989. The traditional story is told from the wolf's point of view.

Steptoe, John. *Mufaro's Beautiful Daughters.* New York: Lothrop, Lee and Shepard Books, 1987. The author bases this story on an African folktale similar to the fairy tale, *Cinderella.*

Taylor, Paula. *Coretta Scott King: A Woman of Peace.* Mankato: Creative Education, 1974. The author presents a brief biography of the wife of the slain Civil Rights leader, Martin Luther King, Jr.

Winter, Jeanette. *Follow the Drinking Gourd.* New York: Alfred A. Knopf, 1988. Based on the song by the same name, this is the fictionalized story of a black family's escape to freedom in Canada just before the Civil War in America.

Van Allsburg, Chris. *Just a Dream.* Boston: Houghton Mifflin, 1990. A young boy's disregard for the environment leads him to have a nightmare about the future.

Wise, William. *Detective Pinkerton and Mr. Lincoln.* New York: E. P. Dutton, 1964. The author presents an account of the assassination attempt on the life of Abraham Lincoln which was thwarted by the private detective Allan Pinkerton in 1860.

4 INFORMATION SKILLS

There are some educators who abhor the term *skills* and would be happy if it were never used to describe the learner standards for the activities that take place in the library media center. This same attitude is partially responsible for the wholesale adoption of whole language instruction and literature based teaching. Learning can be meaningful and entertaining, but the fact remains that there are skills to be taught. The kinds of information skills that can be taught in the library media center evolve from the natural processes of using the resources available there. These skills provide the means to an end, not the final product itself. The library media specialist teaches the use of the card or computer catalog, for instance, to enable the students to find the materials they need, not as an exercise in alphabetizing, filing, or keyboarding, although the lesson will reinforce those skills as well. Students must be made to understand the practical usefulness of these skills if they are truly going to learn them. In many instances, the LMS must *entice* the students into learning, by disguising the skill as a game or activity. Gentle persuasion does not usually work, nor does force. In the lessons included in this chapter, an effort has been made to find some unique approaches to teaching information skills on the topics of arrangement of the various materials in the LMC, the parts of a book, research sources, use of the card or computerized catalog, and the Dewey Decimal System. Many of the lessons use literature as an introduction or as a basis for the skill. A bibliography of children's books used in the lessons is included at the end of the chapter.

Kindergarten

Easy ABC's. Students learn that picture books in the Easy Fiction Section of the LMC are arranged alphabetically by the author's last name by alphabetizing themselves by their last names.

Wild Child. Students practice sequencing skills by acting out the story *Where the Wild Things Are.* They can make *monster* masks to really get into character.

What a Nightmare. After viewing a videotaped version of *There's a Nightmare In My Closet* and then listening to the actual book, students must recall details to make a comparison of the two presentations.

First Grade

Bears' Picnic. Students must put the parts of a familiar bear story, *Corduroy,* in sequential order before the can enjoy a picnic with their teddy bears and the book *Teddy Bears' Picnic.*

Keys to Fiction. In order to *unlock* the Easy Fiction section of the LMC, students practice alphabetizing skills.

Sum of the Parts. After listening to the book *Owliver,* students can play a game by identifying the parts of a book.

Second Grade

Book Backbones. Students study the arrangement of fiction books using their spine labels and practice finding the shelf locations of several titles.

Dictionary of Names. Dictionary use becomes meaningful as students define themselves and make a classroom dictionary for their teacher.

Dinosaur Hunt. A discussion of several books about dinosaurs by the author/illustrator Aliki introduces the students to the nonfiction section of the LMC and shows how to find books there.

Third Grade

Thanksgiving Feasts. The Pilgrims' first Thanksgiving is compared to the modern celebration. Students use simple research skills to discover what the Pilgrims really ate at the first feast.

Fiction Books Relay. Students compete as teams to find books located in the fiction shelves and identify their spine labels. Blank spine label strips are included.

Just Ducky. Using books and songs about ducks, students discover the differences between fiction and nonfiction and create some *duck* books of their own.

Fourth Grade

Bicycle Parts. Parts of a bicycle are compared to parts of a book as students discuss the use and importance of the parts of both.

A Catalog Mystery. Students identify objects in the mystery bag to discover the use of subject cards in the card catalog or subject searches using the computerized catalog.

Dinosaurus Thesaurus. The thesaurus is defined and its use is examined.

Reference Bookmarks. Students are given bookmarks with reference questions they must answer.

Fifth Grade

Dewey Posters. Using magazine pictures, students create collages illustrating the subjects of each Dewey Decimal class.

Maps, Maps, Maps. Using atlases and encyclopedias, students create maps of the states on transparencies and share them with the class.

Pocahontas. Students investigate the two lives of Pocahontas as both an Indian Princess and an English lady and create a display depicting those lives.

Sixth Grade

Biographical Dictionary. Students compare several biographical sources and create a biographical dictionary for the school.

Touring with Dewey. Various aspects of the Japanese culture are introduced to the students as they explore the Dewey Decimal System and discover books about Japan can be found in several areas of nonfiction books.

Tic Tac Toe. Students team up and answer questions about the library media center to try to win a *square* and the game for their team as they review important terms and skills.

Kindergarten	**LIBRARY MEDIA INSTRUCTIONAL PLAN**	DATE_____

Easy ABC's

LMC LEARNER STANDARDS

Orientation & Circulation
1. LMC Areas: INTRODUCE **Circulation Area; Fiction/Easy Section(s); Periodical Section**
2. Vocabulary: INTRODUCE **LMC; media; author; illustrator; title; fiction**
3. INTRODUCE LMC Rules
4. INTRODUCE Local Circulation Procedures
5. INTRODUCE Book Care Rules

Literature Appreciation
1. Fiction
   01. Types: Picture Books
   02. Elements: Plot (sequence)
2. Nonfiction
   01. Folklore (Fairy Tales; Folktales; Holidays; Nursery Rhymes)
   02. Poetry
3. Multicultural Literature
4. Authors/Illustrators
5. Award Books (Caldecott)

Information Skills
1. Parts of a Book: INTRODUCE **front cover; back cover; title; spine**
2. Research: INTRODUCE Comprehension Skills; Sequencing Skills; Recalling Details; Identifying Main Idea; Alphabetical Order

Technology
1. INTRODUCE Proper Use & Care of Appropriate AV Equipment
2. INTRODUCE Viewing & Listening Skills

CURRICULUM CORRELATION

_____

_____

_____

_____

_____

_____

MATERIALS:
Books from the Easy Fiction and Fiction Sections of the LMC
3" x 5" Cards
Marker

FOCUS:
Tell the students that ABC or alphabetical order is very important when finding books in the Library Media Center. Have them recite the alphabet. Explain that the name of the author of a book is also very important. Have the students recall what an author does. *Tell the students that today we'll explore the arrangement of the books on the Easy Fiction Shelves.*

ACTIVITY:
Take the students to the section of the LMC where the Easy Fiction books are shelved. Point out the sign that identifies the section. Ask students what kind of books they might find here. (The students should have already been introduced to the term *fiction* and should be able to recognize these books as *make-believe story books.*)

Explain that many *easy* books are ones that are written for kids just learning how to read and that they usually have lots of pictures but not as many words. They are also called *picture books.* Go to the Fiction Section of the LMC and bring a fiction book to compare to a book from the Easy Fiction Section.

Point out that each shelf is labeled with the letters of the alphabet and that the shelves are in alphabetical order. Point to each shelf as the students say the alphabet. Point out that some letters may identify more than one shelf because there are so many books there that they had to take up two shelves. Tell the students that each book in the LMC belongs on its own special shelf and that the way to find that special shelf is to find out the author's last name. Ask the students if they know the *Curious George* books. Tell them that the author of those books was H. A. Rey. Have them identify *R* as the first letter of the author's last name. Go to the *R* shelf and find a *Curious George* book. (Check in advance to make sure a *Curious George* book is on the shelf. If not, select another familiar author for this demonstration.)

CLOSURE:
Select a very short picture book and read it to the students. When finished have them identify the shelf where the book belongs and return it to the shelf so others can find it later.

EXTENSION:
Tell the students that they will pretend to be books and they will put themselves in ABC order by their last names. Have each student say the first letter of his/her last name. Write the letter on an index card and give it to the student. Have the students hold their cards in front of them so all the students can see the letters. Find the first student and start the line. Then have the students put themselves in order.

NOTES:
Labels for the various sections of the Library Media Center may vary from school to school. Of course, this lesson can be adapted to fit any arrangement.

| Kindergarten | **LIBRARY MEDIA INSTRUCTIONAL PLAN** | DATE_____ |

Wild Child

LMC LEARNER STANDARDS

Orientation & Circulation
1. LMC Areas: INTRODUCE **Circulation Area; Fiction/Easy Section(s); Periodical Section**
2. Vocabulary: INTRODUCE **LMC; media; author, illustrator, title, fiction**
3. INTRODUCE LMC Rules
4. INTRODUCE Local Circulation Procedures
5. INTRODUCE Book Care Rules

Literature Appreciation
1. Fiction
   01. Types: Picture Books
   02. Elements: Plot (sequence)
2. Nonfiction
   01. Folklore (Fairy Tales; Folktales; Holidays; Nursery Rhymes)
   02. Poetry
3. Multicultural Literature
4. Authors/Illustrators
5. Award Books (Caldecott)

Information Skills
1. Parts of a Book: INTRODUCE **front cover; back cover; title; spine**
2. Research: INTRODUCE Comprehension Skills; Sequencing Skills; Recalling Details; Identifying Main Idea; Alphabetical Order

Technology
1. INTRODUCE Proper Uses & Care of Appropriate AV Equipment
2. INTRODUCE Viewing & Listening Skills

MATERIALS:
Filmstrip Imagine That! (Pied Piper); Filmstrip Projector
Book, Where the Wild Things Are by Maurice Sendak
Chalk, Chalkboard, or Vocabulary Board
Extension Project:
Paper Plates, Scissors, Glue, Yarn, Paper and Fabric Scraps

FOCUS:
Ask students if any of them ever have dreams about monsters. Assure them that monsters are not real. Ask the students what word describes books of the imagination or make-believe books in the LMC (fiction). *Tell the students that we're going to see several books of the imagination and discover what makes these books make-believe story books.*

ACTIVITY:
Show the filmstrip. It will introduce the concept of *imagination* through the presentation of several picture books. Afterwards ask students to recall the book about the *Wild Things.*

Show them the book Where the Wild Things Are. Remind them to look carefully at the pictures as you read the book, because the illustrator, Maurice Sendak, won the Caldecott Medal for having the best picture book during the year that this book was published. Point out the words *Caldecott Medal* and *illustrator* on the vocabulary board or write them on the chalkboard.

Read the book to the class. Explain that the monsters, Max and his mother are the *characters* in the story . Show the word *character* and define it as *the people or animals in a story.* Tell the students that they are going to be the *characters* as we act out the story. Have them be *monsters.* Teach them how to roll their eyes, show their *claws* and roar (not scream).

Tell the students that the action of the story is the *plot* and we will act out the *plot.* Show the word *plot* and define it as *what happens in a story.* Have the students sit in a circle on the floor. Select one student to be Max and another to be his mother. The remaining students will be *monsters.*

Max and his mother stand in the center of the circle. Explain to the *monsters* that they are to perform when the story directs them to do so and that they can reach out toward Max, but they cannot move from their positions.

Read the story again, pausing for the characters to act out their parts. The story can be repeated as many times as necessary so that all the students who desire may have a chance at being Max.

CLOSURE
Have the students tell why the story is *make-believe.* Review the definitions of *plot, character, illustrator* and *Caldecott Medal.*

EXTENSION:
Before acting out the story, you can have the students make monster masks using paper plates, yarn and paper or fabric scraps. They can wear these masks during their performance.

NOTES:
You may want to *take this act on the road.* Many teachers do not accompany their students to the LMC. Send the book back to the classroom for the teacher to read as the class performs or allow time to take the children to a nearby classroom where previous arrangements have already been made for them to entertain those students.

| Kindergarten | **LIBRARY MEDIA INSTRUCTIONAL PLAN** | DATE_____ |

What a Nightmare

LMC LEARNER STANDARDS

Orientation & Circulation
1. LMC Areas: INTRODUCE **Circulation Area; Fiction/Easy Section(s); Periodical Section**
2. Vocabulary: INTRODUCE **LMC; media; author; illustrator; title; fiction**
3. INTRODUCE LMC Rules
4. INTRODUCE Local Circulation Procedures
5. INTRODUCE Book Care Rules

Literature Appreciation
1. Fiction
   01. Types: Picture Books
   02. Elements: Plot (sequence)
2. Nonfiction
   01. Folklore (Fairy Tales; Folktales; Holidays; Nursery Rhymes)
   02. Poetry
3. Multicultural Literature
4. Authors/Illustrators
5. Award Books (Caldecott)

Information Skills
1. Parts of a Book: INTRODUCE **front cover; back cover; title; spine**
2. Research: INTRODUCE Comprehension Skills; Sequencing Skills; Recalling Details; Identifying Main Idea; Alphabetical Order

Technology
1. INTRODUCE Proper Use & Care of Appropriate AV Equipment
2. INTRODUCE Viewing & Listening Skills

CURRICULUM CORRELATION

_____
_____
_____
_____
_____
_____
_____
_____

MATERIALS:
Big Book, There's a Nightmare in My Closet by Mercer Mayer
Film, There's a Nightmare in My Closet (Phoenix Films)
VCR
Chalk and Chalkboard or Chart Tablet and Marker
Extension Project:
"Closet Door" Activity Sheet (see next page)
Crayons

FOCUS:
Activate the students' prior knowledge by asking students about their nightmares. Ask if there are ever monsters in their nightmares. Ask if sometimes when they go to bed at night they're a little scared. Explain that those monsters in their nightmares are only imaginary or make-believe. Ask the students to explain the difference between *real* and *make-believe*. Introduce the word *fiction* as make-believe story books. ***Tell the students that today we'll look at a fiction book about nightmares and talk about the difference between real and make-believe.***

ACTIVITY:
Read the big book There's a Nightmare in My Closet.

Tell the students that now we'll look at a film about the same book. Have them watch to see how the film and the book are different.

After the film is over, read the big book again. Have the students point out the similarities and differences between the book and the film.

Have the students tell how they knew that this was a fiction book.

CLOSURE:
Have the students describe the monster that was the boy's nightmare. Ask them to describe the monsters in their nightmares.
        Are they tall or short?
        Are they fat or skinny?
        Are they hairy or scaly?
        What colors are they?
        Are they friendly or mean?
        Do they have horns on their heads?
        Do they have fangs and claws?
Have the students get good pictures in their minds of what their nightmares would look like.

EXTENSION:
Duplicate the Closet Door Activity Sheet and cut it out. Cut around the door except for the side with the *hinges*. Fold the door back along that side so that it appears to open. Fold the paper in half along the dotted line.

Distribute the Activity Sheets and have the students write their names on them. Have each student open the closet door and draw a picture of his/her *nightmare.*

NOTES:
This is a great lesson to correlate with the classroom curriculum when the teachers are teaching about *night*.

_____'s
Nightmare

GRADE 1	LIBRARY MEDIA INSTRUCTIONAL PLAN	DATE_____

Bears' Picnic

LMC LEARNER STANDARDS

Orientation & Circulation
1. LMC Areas: REVIEW **Circulation Area; Fiction/Easy Section(s); Periodical Section**
2. Vocabulary: REVIEW LMC; media; author; illustrator; title; fiction; INTRODUCE **spine label; dictionary**
3. REVIEW LMC Rules
4. REVIEW Local Circulation Procedures/ Check Out Books
5. REVIEW Book Care Rules

Literature Appreciation
1. Fiction
   01. Types: Picture Books
   02. Elements: Plot; Character
2. Nonfiction
   01. Folklore (Fairy Tales; Folktales; Holidays; Nursery Rhymes)
   02. Poetry
3. Multicultural Literature
4. Authors/Illustrators
5. Award Books (Caldecott)

Information Skills
1. Location of Materials: INTRODUCE Location of Fiction Books on Shelves by Spine Label
2. Parts of a Book: REVIEW front cover; back cover; spine; title; INTRODUCE title page
3. Research: REVIEW Comprehension Skills; Sequencing Skills; Recalling Details; Identifying Main Idea; Alphabetical Order; INTRODUCE Identifying Fantasy; Picture Dictionary

Technology
1. REVIEW/INTRODUCE Proper Use & Care of Appropriate AV Equipment
2. REVIEW/INTRODUCE Viewing & Listening Skills

CURRICULUM CORRELATION

Music

_____

_____

_____

_____

_____

MATERIALS:
Bookmarks, Invitation to the Teddy Bears' Picnic (These are given to the students the week before the lesson.) (see next page)
Picnic Supplies (Set the *picnic* up in the LMC before the students arrive.)
Book and Record, The Teddy Bears' Picnic by Jimmy Kennedy, Record Player
Teddy-Bear Shaped Cookies
Book, Corduroy by Don Freeman, Corduroy Stuffed Bear
Story Parts Sentence Strips. Before the lesson, prepare sentence strips labelled with the following story lines:

> Corduroy, the teddy bear, lives in a department store.
> A little girl wants to buy him, but can't because he's missing a button.
> Corduroy looks for his button.
> He finds a button on a bed, but it won't come off.
> He makes a noise and the night watchman finds him.
> The night watchman takes Corduroy back to the toy department.
> The next day, the little girl buys Corduroy.
> She takes Corduroy home and fixes his button.
> Corduroy and the little girl are friends.

Label a strip with the author and title to represent the book's cover and one labelled with the author, title and publisher to represent the title page.
Extension Project: Drawing Paper and Crayons

FOCUS:
Ask how many of the students brought their teddy bears to the picnic. Have the students introduce their bears to the class and sit the bears around the *picnic*. Introduce Corduroy to the students. Many of them will be familiar with his story. *Tell the students that today we'll look carefully at Corduroy's story and then we'll join him and the other bears for a picnic.*

ACTIVITY:
Read the book Corduroy. Have the students retell the events of the story in order. Read the sentence strips and distribute them to the students. Point out the sentence strips that describe the cover of the book and the title page. Ask the students with sentence strips to put themselves in the correct order. Ask them what would come first (Cover) and what would be next (Title Page). Then the story events would follow in the order of the story. Repeat until every child has a chance to participate.

Put Corduroy with the other bears for the picnic. Read the book The Teddy Bears' Picnic. Tell the students that teddy bears are actually named after a former president of the U. S., Theodore *Teddy* Roosevelt, who was president a long time ago, even before their grandparents were alive. Teddy Bears' Picnic was first a musical march, written in 1907. Words were added to it later by Jimmy Kennedy who is listed as the author of the book. Finally, the illustrator Alexandra Day painted pictures to go with the music and the book was created. Play the recording and have the students listen to see if it makes them feel like marching.

CLOSURE:
Remind the students that teddy bears are stuffed animals so they'd move around stiffly without bending their knees and elbows. Have the students imagine what it would be like to jump, walk and run like a teddy bear. Play the recording again and have the students *march* to get in line to return to the classroom. Distribute the cookies.

EXTENSION:
If time allows, let the students illustrate the nine story parts. Write the sentences at the bottom of sheets of drawing paper and let the students draw corresponding pictures. They can hold up their drawings as they line up in sequence.

NOTES:
If a paperback copy of the book Corduroy is available, use the pictures instead of the sentence strips for sequencing the story.

You're
Invited
to a
Teddy Bear
Picnic
in the
LMC
on

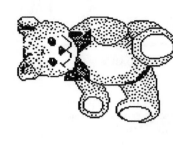

Bring Your
Teddy Bear

You're
Invited
to a
Teddy Bear
Picnic
in the
LMC
on

Bring Your
Teddy Bear

You're
Invited
to a
Teddy Bear
Picnic
in the
LMC
on

Bring Your
Teddy Bear

You're
Invited
to a
Teddy Bear
Picnic
in the
LMC
on

Bring Your
Teddy Bear

GRADE 1	LIBRARY MEDIA INSTRUCTIONAL PLAN	DATE_____

Keys to Fiction

LMC LEARNER STANDARDS

Orientation & Circulation
1. LMC Areas: REVIEW **Circulation Area; Fiction/Easy Section(s)** Periodical Section
2. Vocabulary: REVIEW **LMC; media; author; illustrator; title; fiction;** INTRODUCE **spine label; dictionary**
3. REVIEW LMC Rules
4. REVIEW Local Circulation Procedures/ Check Out Books
5. REVIEW Book Care Rules

Literature Appreciation
1. Fiction
   01. Types: Picture Books
   02. Elements: Plot; Character
2. Nonfiction
   01. Folklore (Fairy Tales; Folktales; Holidays; Nursery Rhymes)
   02. Poetry
3. Multicultural Literature
4. Authors/Illustrators
5. Award Books (Caldecott)

Information Skills
1. Location of Materials: INTRODUCE Location of Fiction Books on Shelves by Spine Label
2. Parts of a Book: REVIEW **front cover; back cover; spine; title;** INTRODUCE **title page**
3. Research: REVIEW Comprehension Skills; Sequencing Skills; Recalling Details; Identifying Main Idea; Alphabetical Order; INTRODUCE Identifying Fantasy; Picture Dictionary

Technology
1. REVIEW/INTRODUCE Proper Use & Care of Appropriate AV Equipment
2. REVIEW/INTRODUCE Viewing & Listening Skills

CURRICULUM CORRELATION

_____ _____

_____ _____

_____ _____

_____ _____

_____ _____

MATERIALS:

Books, When Will I Read? by Miriam Cohen; The Snowy Day by Ezra Jack Keats; Curious George by H. A. Rey; Encore for Eleanor by Bill Peet; Benjamin and Tulip by Rosemary Wells.

Large Key Ring holding Several Different Kinds of Keys

Set of Five Paper Keys for Each Student (Using five different colors of paper, cut out keys shapes using a die cut press or a clip art pattern. Label each key with the last name of one of the authors listed above. Use a separate color for each author. Laminate the *keys*.)

Large Paper Clips, one for Each Student (Open each clip to make a *key ring* for each student.)

Books, The Napping House by Audrey Wood; Freight Train by Donald Crews; Amelia Bedelia by Peggy Parish

Sets of Three Additional Keys (In three different colors and labeled with the last names of the authors listed above)

Extension Project:
Blank Paper Keys

FOCUS:

Hold up the real key ring and ask the students to describe the purpose of keys. Ask them to name some objects that can be opened by keys. They may list *doors, cars, suitcases, trunks,* and *locks.* **Tell the students that we're going to discover a key to unlock a part of the LMC. We'll learn about the key to finding picture books.**

ACTIVITY:

Explain that first we'll hear a story about a first grade student who was really in a hurry to learn how to read. Read the book When Will I Read? Tell the students that when Jim did learn to read, he'd want to go right to the LMC and check out his favorite books, but first he'd have to find them. Ask the student to locate the Easy Fiction Section of the LMC. Remind them that the books there are arranged in a certain order. Most of them will know that they're in alphabetical order according to the author's last name. Show them the spine label of the book. Remind them that they can look there to find the first three letters of the author's last name.

Show the students the other four books: The Snowy Day, Curious George, Encore for Eleanor, and Benjamin and Tulip and ask them to identify the authors.

Distribute the sets of paper keys and key rings. Show the students the last names of the authors printed on each key. Tell the students that they will put the keys in alphabetical order by the authors' last names with the first one on top. Then they'll put them on the key rings in order. You should be able to check for accuracy quickly by noting the order of the colors of the keys.

CLOSURE:

When all of the students are finished, discuss the procedure to follow if the last names of two authors begin with the same letter. Explain that they have to look at the second letter in the name. Distribute the second set of keys. Have the students remove the keys from their key rings and insert the new ones. They have all eight keys on the rings in alphabetical order. Check for accuracy.

EXTENSION:

Give each student a blank paper key to use as a bookmark. Have them write their names, last name first, on the keys. Encourage them to check out a book by an author whose last name begins with the same letter as their own.

NOTES:

Although a lot of preparation is required for this lesson, the materials can be used year after year.

GRADE 1	LIBRARY MEDIA INSTRUCTIONAL PLAN	DATE_____

Sum of the Parts

LMC LEARNER STANDARDS

Orientation & Circulation
1. LMC Areas: REVIEW **Circulation Area;
   Fiction/Easy Section(s); Periodical Section**
2. Vocabulary: REVIEW LMC; **media;
   author; illustrator; title; fiction;**
   INTRODUCE **spine label; dictionary**
3. REVIEW LMC Rules
4. REVIEW Local Circulation Procedures/
   Check Out Books
5. REVIEW Book Care Rules

Literature Appreciation
1. Fiction
   01. Types: Picture Books
   02. Elements: Plot; Character
2. Nonfiction
   01. Folklore (Fairy Tales; Folktales;
   Holidays; Nursery Rhymes)
   02. Poetry
3. Multicultural Literature
4. Authors/Illustrators
5. Award Books (Caldecott)

Information Skills
1. Location of Materials: INTRODUCE
   Location of Fiction Books on Shelves by
   Spine Label
2. Parts of a Book: REVIEW front cover;
   back cover; spine; title; INTRODUCE
   title page
3. Research: REVIEW Comprehension Skills;
   Sequencing Skills; Recalling Details;
   Identifying Main Idea; Alphabetical Order;
   INTRODUCE Identifying Fantasy; Picture
   Dictionary

Technology
1. REVIEW/INTRODUCE Proper Use & Care
   of Appropriate AV Equipment
2. REVIEW/INTRODUCE Viewing &
   Listening Skills

CURRICULUM CORRELATION

_____

_____

_____

_____

_____

_____

MATERIALS:
Books written by Robert Kraus and illustrated by Jose Aruego:
> Owliver, Whose Mouse Are You?, Milton the Early Riser, Come Out and
> Play, Little Mouse, Three Friends, Leo the Late Bloomer, Herman the
> Helper, Musical Max, Mert the Blurt, Another Mouse to Feed

Extension Project:
Set of Five Different Colored Book Shapes for Each Child (These can be cut out using
a die cut machine or traced from a pattern of an open book.)
Pencils, Chalk and Chalkboard or Vocabulary Board

FOCUS:
Have the students identify the terms *author* and *illustrator*. Show the class the covers
of two or three of the books and introduce the author/illustrator team, Robert Kraus
and Jose Aruego. Explain that, although they sometimes work with other authors and
illustrators, they really enjoy creating books together as we can see by looking at all
of these books that have been written by Robert Kraus and illustrated by Jose Aruego.
Explain that each of them has an important part in making a picture book, because the
pictures and the story must go together to make the book. *Tell the students that today
we're going to look at something else in the LMC that has important parts - the parts
of a book.*

ACTIVITY:
Read the book Owliver. Afterwards, ask the students how many of them thought
Owliver would be a lawyer when he grew up. Ask how many thought he'd be an actor.
Ask how many thought he'd be a fireman. Ask the students how many of them have
ever had a part in a play. Remind them that they had to say their parts in the right order
and at the right time. None of the parts could be left out or the play wouldn't make
sense. Explain that books also have parts and that each part has a special job and a
special place. Show the parts of the book in order and demonstrate with a book: *front
cover, title page, story, spine, back cover.* Discuss the following points and
demonstrate with the books. Ask students to recall a time when they were looking
for books on the LMC book shelves. Sometimes when they selected a book, they
were looking a the back cover. They couldn't really tell if they wanted that book by
looking at the back of it. They had to look at the front cover because that's where the
author and title of the book can be found. Explain that if the cover of the book came
off, we'd need the title page to help make a new cover, because it also lists the author,
title and illustrator of the book. Point out that there wouldn't even be a book without
a story. Explain that the spine is the backbone of the book and helps hold the pages
in the book and that it, along with the front and back covers, will protect the pages
of the book.

CLOSURE:
Hold up one of the books and have the students identify its parts.

EXTENSION:
Give each student a set of five different colored *book shapes*. Write the five parts of
a book on the chalkboard or point them out on the vocabulary board. Have the
students write the name of a book part on each *book shape*. Make sure all the students
use the came color for each part: Front Cover (Red), Title Page (Blue), Story
(Yellow), Spine (Green), and Back Cover (Orange). Have the students spread out
their *book shapes* so they can easily grab each one. Call out the parts of the book and
have the student hold up the correct word. Accuracy can be checked by looking at
the colors. Now take a book and turn your back to the students. Tell them that when
you turn around, you'll be showing them a part of the book. They must hold up the
word that describes that book. Watch carefully for the first student to hold up the
correct word and have him/her stand up and say it. Then that student can take your
place, turn his/her back and select a part of the book for the other students to identify.
And so the game continues.

NOTES:

GRADE 2	LIBRARY MEDIA INSTRUCTIONAL PLAN	DATE_____

Book Backbones

LMC LEARNER STANDARDS

Orientation & Circulation
1. LMC Areas: REVIEW **Circulation Area; Fiction/Easy Section(s); Periodical Section;** INTRODUCE **Reference Section; Card/ Computer Catalog; Nonfiction Section; Biography Section**
2. Vocabulary: REVIEW **LMC; media; author; illustrator; title; spine label; fiction; dictionary;** INTRODUCE **fable; biography; nonfiction; fairy tale; table of contents; reference; chapter; card/ computer catalog**
3. REVIEW LMC Rules
4. REVIEW Local Circulation Procedures/ Check Out Books
5. REVIEW Book Care Rules

Literature Appreciation
1. Fiction
   01. Types: Realistic; Mystery & Fantasy
   02. Elements: Plot; Character; Setting
2. Nonfiction
   01. Folklore (Fairy Tales & Fables)
   02. Poetry
   03. Biography
   04. Informational
3. Multicultural Literature
4. Award Books (Caldecott)
5. Authors & Illustrators

Information Skills
1. Location of Materials: REVIEW **Arrangement of Fiction Books;** INTRODUCE **Arrangement of Nonfiction Books & Arrangement of Biography Books**
2. Parts of a Book: REVIEW **front cover; back cover; spine; title; title page;** INTRODUCE **table of contents**
3. Research: REVIEW **Use of Dictionary; Alphabetical Order;** INTRODUCE **Use of Maps & Globes; Use of Tables & Graphs; Differences between Books and Periodicals; Differences Between Fact & Fiction**

Technology
1. REVIEW/INTRODUCE Proper Use & Care of Appropriate AV Equipment
2. REVIEW/INTRODUCE Viewing & Listening Skills

CURRICULUM CORRELATION

_____

_____

_____

_____

_____

_____

MATERIALS:

Spine Label Cards (see next page) These must be made ahead of time, but can be used over and over again. Instead of writing the author and title, you may want to use small pictures of the books from publishers' catalogs. 5" x 8" cards work best.
Transparency of a Spine Label (see next pages)
Overhead Projector, Transparency Pens

FOCUS:

Ask how many of the students know their street addresses. Explain that just as an address tells which house on the block or which apartment in the building is theirs, there is an address on the book that tells its location on the shelf. *Tell the students that we will investigate the arrangement of the Easy Fiction Books.*

ACTIVITY:

Display the transparency of a spine label from an Easy Fiction book and show how it is the same as the spine label on a book. Explain that the top part of the spine label, the *E* tells which section of the LMC the book belongs in - the Easy Fiction Section. Have students find that section of the LMC. This part of the spine label is like the street name of an address. It tells you where to go, but not which house or shelf to go to.

Point out the *Author Letters* located beneath the *E* on the spine label. Show that these are the first three letters of the author's last name. This is like the house number in an address. Easy Fiction books are arranged in ABC order by the author's last name. Go to the Easy Fiction shelves and point out the shelf labels. Look at the transparency and have students decide which shelf that book would go on. Explain that in the Easy Fiction, we only need to look at the first letter on the bottom part of the spine label.

Point out the other spine labels on the transparency and have the students identify the proper shelves for those books. Look at the incomplete spine labels on the transparency. Ask the students to pretend that they are authors and have a few students tell the three author letters that would be on the spine labels of their books. Write the letters on the incomplete spine labels on the transparency.

Distribute spine label cards and have the students slide them into the shelves where the corresponding books would belong. Repeat this *shelving* process a second time.

CLOSURE:

Discuss how ABC order is important in the Library Media Center. Divide the class into groups of three. Mix up the spine label cards and give each group five cards to alphabetize. Have each group share the results with the class.

EXTENSION:

Students in the second grade (and even in first grade and kindergarten) can be taught to re-shelve their own library books when they return them to the LMC. After the students have become acquainted with the arrangement of the Easy Fiction section of the LMC, let them try re-shelving their books. They can put the book in the shelf and stand next to it until the LMS can check to see that it's in the proper location. Later students can be paired to check each other. The books will not be in exact order by author's last name, but they will be on the correct shelf!

NOTES:

Preparation for this lesson may require singing the Alphabet Song or practicing alphabetical order before the lesson begins. The students should be familiar with the alphabet or this lesson will be too frustrating for them.

SPINE LABELS
EASY FICTION BOOKS

E FRE	E DUV	E LOB
<u>Corduroy</u> by Don Freeman	<u>Petunia</u> by Roger Duvoisin	<u>Frog and Toad</u> by Arnold Lobel
E ___	E ___	E ___

Spine Label Card Examples
5" x 8" Cards

The Quilt
by
Ann Jonas

E
JON

Rosie's Walk
by
Pat Hutchins

E
HUT

GRADE 2	LIBRARY MEDIA INSTRUCTIONAL PLAN	DATE_____

Dictionary of Names

LMC LEARNER STANDARDS

Orientation & Circulation
1. LMC Areas: REVIEW **Circulation Area; Fiction/Easy Section(s); Periodical Section;** INTRODUCE **Reference Section; Nonfiction Section; Biography Section; Card/Computer Catalog**
2. Vocabulary: REVIEW **LMC; media; author; illustrator; title; fiction; spine label; dictionary;** INTRODUCE **biography; nonfiction; fable; fairy tale; table of contents; reference; chapter; card/ computer catalog**
3. REVIEW LMC Rules
4. REVIEW Local Circulation Procedures/ Check Out Books
5. REVIEW Book Care Rules

Literature Appreciation
1. Fiction
   01. Types: Realistic; Mystery & Fantasy
   02. Elements: Plot; Character; Setting
2. Nonfiction
   01. Folklore (Fairy Tales & Fables)
   02. Poetry
   03. Biography
   04. Informational
3. Multicultural Literature
4. Award Books (Caldecott)
5. Authors & Illustrators

Information Skills
1. Location of Materials: REVIEW Arrangement of Fiction Books; INTRODUCE Arrangement of Nonfiction Books & Arrangement of Biography Books
2. Parts of a Book: REVIEW **front cover; back cover; spine; title; page;** INTRODUCE **table of contents**
3. Research: REVIEW **Use of Dictionary;** Alphabetical Order; INTRODUCE Use of Maps & Globes; Use of Tables & Graphs; Differences between Books and Periodicals; Differences Between Fact & Fiction

Technology
1. REVIEW/INTRODUCE Proper Use & Care of Appropriate AV Equipment
2. REVIEW/INTRODUCE Viewing & Listening Skills

CURRICULUM CORRELATION

_____
_____
_____
_____
_____

MATERIALS:
Pencils and Paper
Transparency, "Dictionary Entry" (see next page)
Overhead Projector, Transparency Pens
Extension Project: Crayons, Construction Paper, Stapler

FOCUS:
Ask the students what reference book they use when they want to know something about *words*. (They will know to look in a dictionary.) Ask students to recall all the things they can discover about words in a dictionary. They will probably remember at least the following answers:

> How to spell it
> How to say it
> What kind of word it is
> What the word means

Tell the students that we'll look at a word in the dictionary together to find out everything we can about that word. In addition, we will make a class dictionary to give to the classroom teacher.

ACTIVITY:
Show the transparency of the sample dictionary entry. Go over the entry step-by-step, explaining every part. Show the students how the word is divided into syllables with the *dots*. Explain that in some dictionaries, the division of syllables is shown with slashes or spaces. Have the students look at the word in parenthesis and explain the use of the pronunciation key.

Point out the italicized *n* and ask the students what it means. Tell them it is the kind of word that *bicycle* is - a noun. Have them define the word noun. Verify that a bicycle is a *person, place or thing*. Discuss the definition and the sample sentence. Explain that *pl* is the abbreviation for *plural*. Have them spell the plural form of *bicycle*.

Tell the students that the word *bicycle* can also be a verb, or a word that shows action as indicated by the italicized *v*. Read the sample sentence and the definition. Point out the other forms of the verb listed.

CLOSURE:
Explain to the students that they are making a classroom dictionary and each entry will be a student's name. Using a blank transparency, write your name (or the principal's name). Divide the name into syllables, write the phonetic spelling using the pronunciations key. Put an *n*, because you are a person place or thing and write a description of yourself. Give each student a piece of paper and help them define themselves, using their first names. Leave the Pronunciation Key on the Overhead Projector for reference. (This will be the most difficult part for the students and you may want to omit it.)

EXTENSION:
If time allows, have the students draw pictures of themselves. When the students are finished, ask them how the words in a dictionary are arranged. They should know about alphabetical order. Have them line up alphabetically by their first names and collect the papers so they'll be in alphabetical order. Staple the pages together, add a cover of construction paper. Title the book *Dictionary of Students*. Add the teacher's name and the date. Give the book to the teacher as a gift. Have the students recall, for their classroom teacher, the information available in a dictionary. They should be able to recall seven items: spelling, number of syllables, pronunciation, kind of word, definition, sample sentence, and plural spelling.

NOTES:

Dictionary Entry

Bi·cy·cle (bī′ sĭ kəl) *n.* a kind of transportation with two wheels, moved by foot pedaling and guided by handlebar steering. [He rides a bicycle to school.]

pl. **Bicycles**

v. to ride a bicycle [She bicycled to the park.]

Bicycled; Bicycling

Pronunciation Key

ă	bat	ō	no	ʉ	purr
ā	ape	ô	saw	ch	chill
ä	dot	ŏŏ	book	sh	she
ĕ	ten	ōō	boot	th	thick
ē	be	oi	boil	*th*	that
ĭ	mit	ou	out	zh	vision
ī	lie	ŭ	up	ə	bug

GRADE 2	LIBRARY MEDIA INSTRUCTIONAL PLAN	DATE_____

Dinosaur Hunt

LMC LEARNER STANDARDS

Orientation & Circulation
1. LMC Areas: REVIEW **Circulation Area;**
   Fiction/Easy Section(s); Periodical Section;
   Card/Computer Catalog; INTRODUCE
   Reference Section; Nonfiction Section;
   Biography Section
2. Vocabulary: REVIEW LMC; media;
   author; illustrator; title; fiction; spine label;
   dictionary; INTRODUCE biography;
   nonfiction; fable; fairy tale; table of contents;
   reference; chapter; card/computer catalog
3. REVIEW LMC Rules
4. REVIEW Local Circulation Procedures/Check
   Out Books
5. REVIEW Book Care Rules

Literature Appreciation
1. Fiction
   01. Types: Realistic; Mystery & Fantasy
   02. Elements: Plot; Character; Setting
2. Nonfiction
   01. Folklore (Fairy Tales & Fables)
   02. Poetry
   03. Biography
   04. Informational
3. Multicultural Literature
4. Award Books (Caldecott)
5. Authors & Illustrators

Information Skills
1. Location of Materials: REVIEW Arrangement
   of Fiction Books; INTRODUCE Arrangement
   of Biography & Arrangement of Nonfiction
   Books
2. Parts of a Book: REVIEW **front cover; back
   cover; spine; title; title page;** INTRODUCE
   table of contents
3. Research: REVIEW Use of Dictionary;
   Alphabetical Order; INTRODUCE Use of
   Maps & Globes; Use of Tables & Graphs;
   Differences between Books and Periodicals;
   Differences Between Fact & Fiction

Technology
1. REVIEW/INTRODUCE Proper Use & Care of
   Appropriate AV Equipment
2. REVIEW/INTRODUCE Viewing & Listening
   Skills

CURRICULUM CORRELATION

Science

_____

_____

_____

_____

_____

MATERIALS:

Filmstrip, How to Hunt for Dinosaurs (Eye Gate Media)
Books by Aliki, Dinosaurs Are Different
            Dinosaur Bones
            Digging Up Dinosaurs
            My Visit to the Dinosaurs
            Fossils Tell of Long Ago
Book, Meet the Author and Illustrators by Deborah Kovacs and James Preller
Extension Project:
Butterscotch, Chocolate and Vanilla Instant Pudding
Milk; Small Animal-Shaped Cookies; Whipped Topping
Large Clear Glass Bowl; Serving Spoon; Paper Cups and Spoons for Students

FOCUS:

Ask the students if they have been to a museum to look at dinosaur fossils. Define
fossil. Ask how many of them like to read about dinosaurs. See how many of them
have read a *fiction* book about dinosaurs. Define *fiction*. Have the students recall
what made the book *fiction*. Ask the students how many of them have read *nonfiction*
books about dinosaurs. Have them define *nonfiction* and point out the Nonfiction
Section of the LMC. *Explain that we will discuss how to find books about dinosaurs
in the nonfiction section of the LMC and discover an author/Illustrator who loves
dinosaurs as much as second graders do!*

ACTIVITY:

Show the filmstrip. Afterwards, ask the students where to look to find out what books
about dinosaurs are in the LMC.   Define the *card/computer catalog* as a guide or
index to all the materials in the LMC.   Have a student look up the subject
DINOSAURS in the card or computer catalog and tell the class the *call number* for
the book. Define *call number*. Point out to the class that in the Nonfiction Section,
most of the books about the same subject are shelved together and have the same
number. Explain that they may want to remember the number for books about
dinosaurs is 567.9 because books in the 500 section are about science, including
animals.

Show the students the picture of Aliki. Explain that she is both an author and an
illustrator. She lives in London with her husband, Franz Brandenberg, who is also
an author. If time allows, read the article about Aliki in the book Meet the Authors
and Illustrators.

Show the books by Aliki and read Dinosaur Bones. Point out that the covers to Aliki's
books may look like story books, but they give us information about dinosaurs so we
know that they're nonfiction books. Show the students the spine label and identify
the call number.

CLOSURE:

Review *fiction, nonfiction, card/computer catalog, author, illustrator,* and *call
number.*

EXTENSION:

In the classroom or on another day have the students help you or the classroom teacher
mix up the instant pudding. Remind the students that the earth is made up of layers
of rock and dirt and that fossils of dinosaurs were found in the different layers that
were formed over a period of millions of years. Put a layer of pudding in the bottom
of the bowl. Place some cookies on top of the pudding, making sure that some are
at the very edge so they will show through the glass bowl as the pudding is layered
on. Tell the students that the cookies represent dinosaurs whose bones were
fossilized. Continue to alternate the pudding in layers putting cookies in between
each layer. Top with a layer of whipped topping and *dig in for some tasty fossils.*

NOTES:

GRADE 3	LIBRARY MEDIA INSTRUCTIONAL PLAN	DATE_____

Thanksgiving Feasts

LMC LEARNER STANDARDS

Orientation & Circulation
1. LMC Areas: REVIEW **Circulation Area; Fiction/Easy Section(s); Periodical Section; Reference Section; Nonfiction Section; Biography Section; Card/Computer Catalog**
2. Vocabulary: REVIEW **media; reference; fiction; nonfiction; periodicals; chapter;** INTRODUCE **publisher; call number; almanac; copyright date; atlas**
3. REVIEW LMC Rules
4. REVIEW Local Circulation Procedures/ Check Out Books
5. REVIEW Book Care Rules

Literature Appreciation
1. Fiction
   01. Types: Mystery; Realistic
   02. Elements: Plot; Character & Setting
2. Nonfiction
   01. Folklore (Fables, Folktales, Fairy Tales)
   02. Poetry
   03. Biography
   04. Informational
3. Multicultural Literature
4. Authors/Illustrators
5. Award Books (Caldecott, Greenaway)

Information Skills
1. Location of Materials: REVIEW/EXTEND Arrangement of Fiction Books; Arrangement of Nonfiction Books & Arrangement of Biography Books
2. Parts of a Book; REVIEW **table of contents, title page** INTRODUCE **glossary; index**
3. Research: REVIEW /EXTEND Use of Dictionary; Alphabetical Order; INTRODUCE Use of Encyclopedia; Use of Periodicals; Use of Special Reference Books; Use of Atlas
4. Card/Computer Catalog: INTRODUCE Types of Cards/Searches & Card/Record Information

Technology
1. REVIEW /INTRODUCE Proper Uses & Care of Appropriate AV Equipment
2. REVIEW /INTRODUCE Viewing & Listening Skills

CURRICULUM CORRELATION

Social Studies

_____

_____

_____

_____

_____

MATERIALS:
Book, Oh, What a Thanksgiving by Steven Kroll
Poem, "If I Were a Pilgrim Child" (Baseball cap and Pilgrim's hat are optional)
Transparency "Thanksgiving Today/Pilgrim's Thanksgiving" (see next page)
Overhead Projector and Transparency Pens
Book, Don't Eat Too Much Turkey by Miriam Cohen (Optional)
Extension Project:
Encyclopedias, Nonfiction Books, Periodicals for Research

FOCUS:
Ask several students to share the way their families celebrate the Thanksgiving holiday. Have them tell whatever background information they already know about the original Thanksgiving feast. Find Plymouth, Massachusetts on a map of the U.S. *Tell the students that we'll compare the Pilgrim's Thanksgiving with today's Thanksgiving celebrations.*

ACTIVITY:
Introduce the vocabulary: *fled, voyage, harbor, thatched roof, musket, harvest, bountiful, survivors,* and venison. Read the book Oh, What a Thanksgiving.

Using the transparency, contrast and compare past and current Thanksgiving celebrations and life-styles. Discuss houses, foods, clothing, getting food, cooking, fun activities and purpose of the feast. Write the students' responses on the transparency.

Read the poem "If I Were a Pilgrim Child." Discuss the vocabulary: *bog, stump, crimson, clasp, platter, wild game,* and *moccasins.* If time allows, have the students take turns individually reading the Pilgrim's part and the modern child's part. Have a Pilgrim's hat and a baseball cap for the readers to wear to set the mood.

Discuss the meaning of Thanksgiving for the Pilgrims and for us today. Tell the students that originally it was a feast of a bountiful harvest or a good crop. Thanksgiving was held almost every year afterwards, but at different times of the year. It wasn't until 1941 that Congress officially made Thanksgiving a legal federal holiday to be celebrated annually on the fourth Thursday in November.

CLOSURE:
Have some of the students share the various ways their families celebrate Thanksgiving. There will be many types of celebrations from elaborate dinners at Grandmother's house to lunches eaten at the cafeteria. A humorous look can be found in the picture book Don't Eat Too Much Turkey in which first graders argue about what food to cook for their make-believe Thanksgiving dinner.

EXTENSION:
Ask the students to find out if the Pilgrims had cranberry sauce and pumpkin pie which are usually served at traditional Thanksgiving dinners today. (The students may not have traditional food at their dinner, but restaurants and cafeterias will always have these two items on their Thanksgiving menus.) The students can look up information in the encyclopedia, in holiday books about Thanksgiving, in American history books or in magazines, whatever is available in the LMC collection. The answer, in case they can't find it, is that the Pilgrims did not have cranberry sauce although there were cranberries growing in the area. They did not have pumpkin pies because they did not have the sugar needed to make them. They ate meat pies in those times.

NOTES:
With the extension project, this lesson might be completed in two sessions. Look for the answer to the question about cranberries and pumpkin pie in advance. If you cannot find it in your LMC, borrow a book from the public library. One answer can be found in the book If You Sailed on the *Mayflower* by Ann McGovern.

THANKSGIVING TODAY	PILGRIM'S THANKSGIVING
Homes	
Food	
Getting Food	
Cooking	
Clothing	
Fun Activities	
Purpose of the Feast	
Other	

GRADE 3	LIBRARY MEDIA INSTRUCTIONAL PLAN	DATE_____

Fiction Books Relay

LMC LEARNER STANDARDS

Orientation & Circulation
1. LMC Areas: REVIEW **Circulation Area; Fiction/Easy Section(s); Periodical Section; Reference Section; Nonfiction Section; Biography Section; Card/Computer Catalog**
2. Vocabulary: REVIEW **media; reference; fiction; nonfiction; periodicals; chapter;** INTRODUCE **publisher; call number; almanac; copyright date; atlas**
3. REVIEW LMC Rules
4. REVIEW Local Circulation Procedures/ Check Out Books
5. REVIEW Book Care Rules

Literature Appreciation
1. Fiction
   01. Types: Mystery; Realistic
   02. Elements: Plot; Character & Setting
2. Nonfiction
   01. Folklore (Fables, Folktales, Fairy Tales)
   02. Poetry
   03. Biography
   04. Informational
3. Multicultural Literature
4. Authors/Illustrators
5. Award Books (Caldecott, Greenaway)

Information Skills
1. Location of Materials: REVIEW/EXTEND **Arrangement of Fiction Books;** Arrangement of Nonfiction Books & Arrangement of Biography Books
2. Parts of a Book REVIEW **table of contents, title page;** INTRODUCE **glossary; index**
3. Research: REVIEW /EXTEND Use of Dictionary; **Alphabetical Order** INTRODUCE Use of Encyclopedia; Use of Periodicals; Use of Special Reference Books; Use of Atlas
4. Card/Computer Catalog: INTRODUCE Types of Cards/Searches & Card/Record Information

Technology
1. REVIEW /INTRODUCE Proper Use & Care of Appropriate AV Equipment
2. REVIEW /INTRODUCE Viewing & Listening Skills

CURRICULUM CORRELATION

_____

_____

_____

_____

MATERIALS:

Twenty paper spines - strips of paper, each typed with a book title and author's full name, to resemble book spines. Strips can be laminated, but the LMS may want to keep blank strips and write in titles of books that are available for use at the time of the game. Some books are always checked out and the student must be able to find the book on the shelf. (see next page)

Two *paper spines* with the note "Congratulations! Your team has found all the Spine Labels. Now put them in alphabetical order by the authors' last names!" (see next page)

Pencils

FOCUS:

Ask students what the information on the spine label of a book is called *(call number)*. Remind students that the top part of the *call number* tells what section of the LMC the book belongs in and the bottom part tells what shelf the book belongs on. *Explain that today we'll take a look at the call numbers of fiction books.* Remind students that fiction books are shelved alphabetically by the authors' last names. Give some examples to make sure students can identify the first three letters of the author's last name.

ACTIVITY:

Before the lesson, the LMS will *plant* the paper book spines in the book pockets of various books in the Fiction Section of the LMC and make a note of which books are used. In the last book to be found by each team, place a note which tells the students they have found all ten *paper spines* and they should now put them in alphabetical order. NOTE: The *paper spines* should not match the book that they are placed in. They are to direct the student to another book.

This is a relay. Divide the students into two teams. Give the first student the first *paper spine*. The student reads the author and title and goes to the shelves to find that book.

When the book is located, the student writes the call number on the spine label of the *paper spine* for the book he/she has found. He/She gets the *paper spine* from the book pocket of the book that has been found and hands it to the next student in line. He/She holds on to the *paper spine* with the call number written on it.

The second student must take that *paper spine,* find the book, write in the call number, get another *paper spine* and pass it to the next student.

CLOSURE:

When a team has collected all ten of their *paper spines* and put them in order, the LMS checks for correct order. The first team finished is the winner.

EXTENSION:

As an extension, have each student show the book to the class once it has been located. The student can read the author and the title to the class. This is a great opportunity to expose the students to some books which are rarely checked out.

NOTES:

To be successful, this lesson requires some careful planning. First place the final *paper spines* (the one that tells the team they are finished) in a book. Then write the title and author of that book on a *paper spine* and put it in the next book and so on until ten books have *paper spines* hidden in their book pockets. The last paper spine should be left to start the game with. Repeat this process for each team in the relay.

Scrambled

Eggs for

Breakfast

_by_

Jamie Gilson

Congratulations! Your team has found all the Spine Labels.

Now put them in Alphabetical Order by the authors' last names.

GRADE 3	LIBRARY MEDIA INSTRUCTIONAL PLAN	DATE_____

Just Ducky

LMC LEARNER STANDARDS

Orientation & Circulation
1. LMC Areas: REVIEW **Circulation Area;
   Fiction/Easy Section(s); Periodical Section;
   Reference Section; Nonfiction Section;
   Biography Section; Card/Computer Catalog**
2. Vocabulary: REVIEW **media; reference;
   fiction; nonfiction; periodicals; chapter;**
   INTRODUCE **publisher; call number;
   almanac; copyright date; atlas**
3. REVIEW **LMC Rules**
4. REVIEW **Local Circulation Procedures/
   Check Out Books**
5. REVIEW **Book Care Rules**

Literature Appreciation
1. Fiction
   01. Types: Mystery; Realistic
   02. Elements: Plot; Character & Setting
2. Nonfiction
   01. Folklore (Fables, Folktales, Fairy Tales)
   02. Poetry
   03. Biography
   04. Informational
3. Multicultural Literature
4. Authors/Illustrators
5. Award Books (Caldecott, Greenaway)

Information Skills
1. Location of Materials: REVIEW/EXTEND
   Arrangement of Fiction Books; Arrangement
   of Nonfiction Books & Arrangement of
   Biography Books
2. Parts of a Book; REVIEW **table of contents,
   title page;** INTRODUCE **glossary; index**
3. Research: REVIEW /EXTEND Use of
   Dictionary; Alphabetical Order; INTRODUCE
   Use of Encyclopedia; Use of Periodicals; Use
   of Special Reference Books; Use of Atlas
4. Card/Computer Catalog: INTRODUCE Types
   of Cards/Searches & Card/Record Information

Technology
1. REVIEW /INTRODUCE Proper Use & Care
   of Appropriate AV Equipment
2. REVIEW /INTRODUCE Viewing &
   Listening Skills

CURRICULUM CORRELATION

Science

Music

_____

_____

_____

_____

MATERIALS:

Fiction Books: The Ugly Duckling by Hans Christian Anderson; The Story about Ping by Marjorie Flack; Angus and the Ducks by Marjorie Flack; Chick and the Duckling by Mirra Ginsburg; Have You Seen My Duckling? by Nancy Tafuri; Little Wood Duck, by Brian Wildsmith; Make Way for Ducklings by Robert McCloskey.
Nonfiction Books: A First Look at Ducks, Geese and Swans by Millicent Selsam; A Duckling Is Born by Hans-Heinrich Isenbart; Ducklings by Kate Petty; Ducks Don't Get Wet by Augusta Goldin.
Encyclopedias
Recordings, Rise and Shine and Everything Goes by Raffi; Record Player
Construction Paper, Stapler

FOCUS:

Play the record and have the students sing the song Five Little Ducks or Little White Duck. Have students recall some *duck* stories they've heard. Then have them share facts they know about ducks. ***Explain that today we'll discover some differences between stories about ducks and facts about ducks.***

ACTIVITY:

Read the book The Chick and the Duckling. Explain that although the book is fiction, we can get some information about the habits of ducks from the book (they hatch from eggs, they are birds, they eat worms and they can swim). Have the students recall some other stories about ducks they have read or heard. Show the other picture books about ducks and ask which ones they're familiar with.

Ask students what kind of books they would use if they wanted to find out some facts about ducks. Ask if any of the students have read any nonfiction books about ducks. Show the students the nonfiction books and read a page or two of one of one of them.

Ask the students where else in the LMC they could look to find factual information about ducks. Point out the Reference Section of the LMC and remind the students that is where the encyclopedias are shelved. Have the students identify the encyclopedia as a set of reference books containing factual information on almost any subject. Ask students how the books or volumes of the encyclopedia are arranged. Have a student find a volume of the encyclopedia that would contain information about ducks. Read a little of the entry and show the students how the information is arranged and what kind of facts about ducks are included.

Tell the class that we're going to write two books about ducks. Each student will write a page of one of the books. Divide the students into four groups. Have the students in two of the groups write and illustrate fictional stories about ducks. Give them the picture books for ideas. Have the students in the other two groups write factual articles about ducks. Give them the encyclopedias and nonfiction books for ideas. Remind the students not to *copy* from any of the books. They must write in their own words and draw their own pictures.

CLOSURE:

When the students are finished, collect their work, staple the pages together into two groups, fiction and nonfiction. Make covers with appropriate titles and give the books to the classroom teacher.

EXTENSION:

Extend this theme into science and math lessons in the classroom by hatching a duck egg, observing, measuring, recording and reporting on the project. The duckling could be taken to local park or zoo after it has hatched.

NOTES:

GRADE 4	LIBRARY MEDIA INSTRUCTIONAL PLAN	DATE_____

Bicycle Parts

LMC LEARNER STANDARDS

Orientation & Circulation
1. LMC Areas: REVIEW **Circulation Area;
   Fiction/Easy Section(s); Periodical Section;
   Reference Section; Nonfiction Section;
   Biography Section; Card/Computer Catalog**
2. Vocabulary: REVIEW **media; reference;
   fiction; nonfiction; periodicals; publisher;
   biography; atlas; almanac; call number;
   copyright date;** INTRODUCE **unabridged
   dictionary; thesaurus; verso**
3. REVIEW LMC Rules
4. REVIEW Local Circulation Procedures/Check
   Out Books
5. REVIEW Book Care Rules

Literature Appreciation
1. Fiction
   01. Types: Historical, Realistic;
   Humorous; Adventure
   02. Elements: Character; Plot; Setting
2. Nonfiction
   01. Folklore (Fables, Folktales, Fairy Tales)
   02. Poetry
   03. Biography
   04. Informational
3. Multicultural Literature
4. Authors/Illustrators
5. Award Books (Newbery; Coretta Scott King)

Information Skills
1. Location of Materials: REVIEW / EXTEND
   Arrangement of Fiction Books; Arrangement
   of Nonfiction Books & Arrangement of
   Biography Books; INTRODUCE
   Arrangement of Audiovisual Materials
2. Parts of a Book: REVIEW **table of contents;
   title page; glossary; index;** INTRODUCE
   dedication
3. Research: REVIEW/EXTEND Alphabetical
   Order; Use of the Encyclopedia; Use of the
   Dictionary; Use of Periodicals; Use of Special
   Reference Books ; INTRODUCE Use of
   Atlas; Use of Almanac; Children's Magazine
   Guide
4. Card/Computer Catalog: REVIEW /EXTEND
   Types of Cards/Searches & Card/Record
   Information

Technology
1. REVIEW/INTRODUCE Proper Use & Care
   of Appropriate AV Equipment & Software
2. REVIEW/INTRODUCE Viewing & Listening
   skills

CURRICULUM CORRELATION

_____

_____
_____
_____
_____

MATERIALS:

Transparencies, "Parts of a Bicycle" and "Parts of a Book" (see next pages)
Filmstrip, The Right Book for You, Part 1: Getting Started (Cheshire)
Overhead Projector and Transparency Pens
10 or 12 Books Containing the Appropriate Book Parts (Two books per table)
Activity Sheet, "Crossword Puzzle - Parts of a Book" (see next pages)

FOCUS:

Find out how many of the students have bicycles. Have the students describe the step-by-step process of riding a bicycle. Ask the students if a person who had never seen a bicycle could follow their directions. If a person didn't know the parts of a bicycle, he/she couldn't very well follow the directions to learn to ride one. *Tell the students that just like knowing about the parts of a bicycle can help you learn how to ride one, knowing about the parts of a book can help you find the information that you need.*

ACTIVITY:

Show the students the transparency of the bicycle and have them identify the following parts: *seat, handlebars, handbrakes, pedals, spokes, chains, gears, gearshift* and *frame*. The students may want to identify other parts.

Explain that knowing about book parts is just as important as important as knowing how to find books in the LMC. Each book part, just like each bicycle part, has a special function that is important to the use of the book.

Show the filmstrip Getting Started. It's about a student who didn't have a clue as to finding a book he'd enjoy reading. Afterwards, explain that if Peter had known more about books he wouldn't have wasted so much time looking for the right book.

Show the students the transparency of the book parts. Point out each part and have the students look at the books on their tables to see if those books have the various parts. Give a brief definition of each part. (See the Crossword Puzzle for possible definitions.)

CLOSURE:

Distribute the crossword puzzles and allow the students to complete them in the LMC, if there is time, or the students can take the puzzles back to the classroom and complete them at home.

ANSWERS: *Down,* 1. Flyleaf; 2. Appendix; 4. Glossary; 5. Front Cover; 7. Index;
              9. Contents; 11. Spine Label; 12. Dedication
           Across, 3. Bibliography; 6. Spine; 8. Forward; 10. Body; 13. Preface;
              14. Title Page; 15. Back Cover

EXTENSION:

If time allows, continue with the analogy between bicycles and books by discussing rules of bicycle safety. Make the transition from bicycle safety to book safety. Lead the students in a discussion of rules of proper book care.

NOTES:

EAGLE VALLEY LIBRARY DIST.
BOX 240/EAGLE, CO 81631
(970)328-8800

Parts of a Bicycle

Parts of a Book

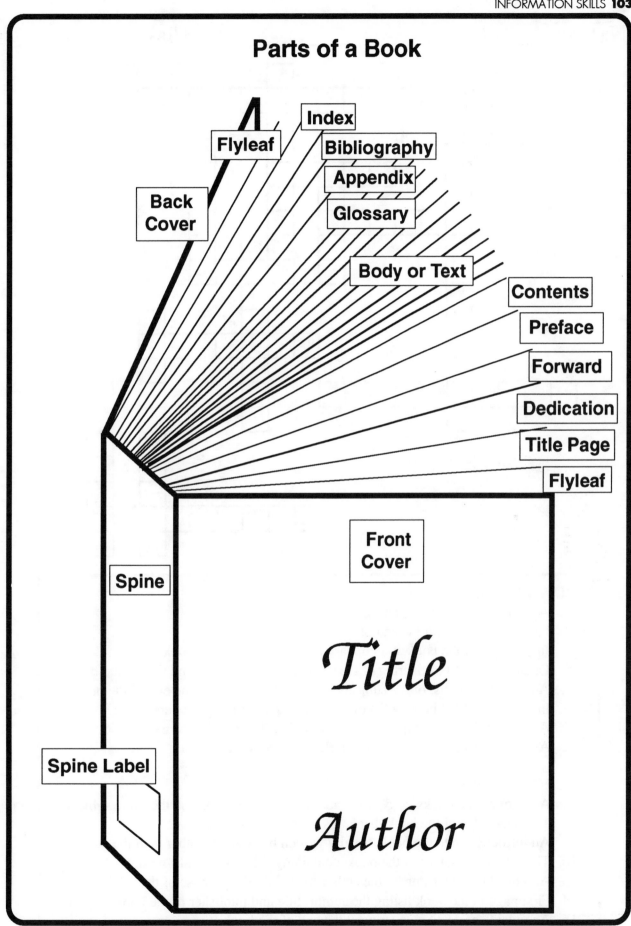

Name: _____ **Class:** _____

Parts of a Book
Crossword Puzzle

DOWN CLUES
1. A blank page at the beginning and end of the book
2. Extra information at the end of the book
4. In the back of the book, a dictionary of words used in the book
5. Outside protective covering of the book listing the author and title of the book
7. An alphabetical list of the subjects in the book, located at the end of the book
9. In the front of the book, a list of the chapters and their page numbers
11. A small label on the edge of the book, telling the shelf location of the book
12. A message from the author as a mark of respect or affection

ACROSS CLUES
3. A list of all the books used by the author or a list of books on the same subject
6. The back edge of the book that holds the pages together
8. An introduction to the book, usually written by someone other than the author
10. The text or main part of the book, containing the story or information
13. An introduction written by the author to explain the purpose of the book
14. First page in the book listing the author, title and publisher of the book
15. An outside protective covering at the end of the book

GRADE 4	LIBRARY MEDIA INSTRUCTIONAL PLAN	DATE_____

A Catalog Mystery

LMC LEARNER STANDARDS

Orientation & Circulation
1. LMC Areas: REVIEW **Circulation Area; Fiction/Easy Section(s); Periodical Section; Reference Section; Biography Section; Nonfiction Section; Card/Computer Catalog**
2. Vocabulary: REVIEW **media; reference; fiction; nonfiction; periodicals; publisher; biography; atlas; almanac; call number; copyright date;** INTRODUCE **unabridged dictionary; thesaurus; verso**
3. REVIEW LMC Rules
4. REVIEW Local Circulation Procedures/Check Out Books
5. REVIEW Book Care Rules

Literature Appreciation
1. Fiction
   01. Types: Historical, Realistic; Humorous; Adventure
   02. Elements: Character; Plot; Setting
2. Nonfiction
   01. Folklore (Fables, Folktales, Fairy Tales)
   02. Poetry
   03. Biography
   04. Informational
3. Multicultural Literature
4. Authors/Illustrators
5. Award Books (Newbery; Coretta Scott King)

Information Skills
1. Location of Materials: REVIEW / EXTEND Arrangement of Fiction Books; Arrangement of Nonfiction Books & Arrangement of Biography Books; INTRODUCE Arrangement of Audiovisual Materials
2. Parts of a Book: REVIEW **table of contents; title page; glossary, index;** INTRODUCE **dedication**
3. Research: REVIEW/EXTEND Alphabetical Order; Use of the Encyclopedia; Use of the Dictionary; Use of Periodicals; Use of Special Reference Books ; INTRODUCE Use of Atlas; Use of Almanac; Children's Magazine Guide
4. Card/Computer Catalog: REVIEW /EXTEND Types of Cards/Searches & Card/Record Information

Technology
1. REVIEW/INTRODUCE Proper Use & Care of Appropriate AV Equipment & Software
2. REVIEW/INTRODUCE Viewing & Listening Skills

CURRICULUM CORRELATION

Language Arts

_____

_____

_____

_____

_____

MATERIALS:
Mystery Bag (Paper Bag) with Six Objects (Valentine Card; Rose; Easter Bunny; Blue Jay; Origami Butterfly; Picture of Abraham Lincoln)
Paper and Pencils for Students
Transparency of Card Catalog or Computer Catalog Search Screen
Overhead Projector, 6 Blank Transparency Sheets and Transparency Pens

FOCUS:
Students have already been introduced to the Card/Computer Catalog and know there are three main kinds of cards/searches available. Have the students name the three kinds of cards/searches. *Tell the students that today we're going to concentrate on the Subject Cards or Subject Searches.* Ask students to define *subject*.

ACTIVITY:
Distribute pencils and paper to students. Explain that in your *Mystery Bag* there are several objects for them to identify. Tell the students that you'll show the object for 30 seconds and they're to write down *exactly* what they see. Reveal each object and return it to the bag.

After all the objects have been shown, remove them one at a time from the bag and have students share their written responses. Write the responses on a transparency, one object per sheet. Point out that there were many different words to describe the various items.

Explain that students will encounter this same situation when they want to find a book by its subject in the card or computer catalog. Many different words can describe similar or the same subjects. It is important to know exactly what you're looking for, but to know other names that might describe the subject.

Explain that the objects represent books you're looking for in the LMC. Take one of the objects, the Easter Bunny, and look at the list of student responses. These may include: *rabbit; bunny; Easter Rabbit; Easter Bunny; stuffed animals; toy;* or *animal*. Tell the students that what you're really looking for is a book about rabbits. Ask them which of those words they'd try in the card catalog.

Tell them if they look for any of the words other than *rabbit,* they probably wouldn't find anything. Explain that usually scientific names of objects are used, rather that nicknames (*rabbit* instead of *bunny*). Explain that usually general terms are used (*rabbit* instead of *Easter Rabbit*).

Try looking up *rabbits* in the card/computer catalog. Discuss the card/record.

CLOSURE:
Divide the students into five groups and give each group an object from the bag and the transparency sheet that describes the object. Tell them to work in groups to decide what book subjects their objects represent. Then they should decide which word they'd look up in the card/computer catalog. Have each group present their choices and discuss their answers.

EXTENSION:
If time allows, have the groups go to the card/computer catalog and to the bookshelves to try to find a book about their objects.

NOTES:
This lesson is can be used to demonstrate similarities between the card and computer catalog when students are making that transition

GRADE 4	LIBRARY MEDIA INSTRUCTIONAL PLAN	DATE_____

Dinosaurus Thesaurus

LMC LEARNER STANDARDS

Orientation & Circulation
1. LMC Areas: REVIEW **Circulation Area; Fiction/Easy Section(s); Periodical Section; Reference Section; Nonfiction Section; Card/Computer Catalog Biography Section; Card/Computer Catalog**
2. Vocabulary: REVIEW **media; reference; fiction; nonfiction; periodicals; publisher; biography; atlas; almanac; call number; copyright date;** INTRODUCE **unabridged dictionary; thesaurus; verso**
3. REVIEW LMC Rules
4. REVIEW Local Circulation Procedures/Check Out Books
5. REVIEW Book Care Rules

Literature Appreciation
1. Fiction
   01. Types: Historical, Realistic, Humorous, Adventure
   02. Elements: Character; Plot; Setting
2. Nonfiction
   01. Folklore (Fables, Folktales, Fairy Tales)
   02. Poetry
   03. Biography
   04. Informational
3. Multicultural Literature
4. Authors/Illustrators
5. Award Books (Newbery; Coretta Scott King)

Information Skills
1. Location of Materials: REVIEW / EXTEND Arrangement of Fiction Books; Arrangement of Nonfiction Books & Arrangement of Biography Books; INTRODUCE Arrangement of Audiovisual Materials
2. Parts of a Book: REVIEW **table of contents; title page; glossary, index;** INTRODUCE **dedication**
3. Research: REVIEW/EXTEND Alphabetical Order; Use of the Encyclopedia; Use of the Dictionary; Use of Periodicals; Use of Special Reference Books ; INTRODUCE Use of Atlas; Use of Almanac; Children's Magazine Guide
4. Card/Computer Catalog: REVIEW /EXTEND Types of Cards/Searches & Card/Record Information

Technology
1. REVIEW/INTRODUCE Proper Use & Care of Appropriate AV Equipment & Software
2. REVIEW/INTRODUCE Viewing & Listening Skills

CURRICULUM CORRELATION

_____

_____

_____

_____

MATERIALS:
Book, Big Old Bones by Carol and Donald Carrick
Transparency, "Dinosaurus Thesaurus" (See next page)
Overhead Projector, Transparency Pens
Several Thesauri of Various Levels (One for Each Table of Students)
Extension Project:
A Picture of dinosaurs in their natural habitat (Use a picture from a book about dinosaurs or a poster of dinosaurs.)
Pencils and Paper

FOCUS:
Have the students name every kind of dinosaur that they can recall. Ask how the dinosaurs got those names. Perhaps when the fossils were discovered the dinosaur's name was carved on each bone. *Tell the students that we're going to discover something about dinosaurs and their relationship to a certain reference book in the LMC.*

ACTIVITY:
Introduce and read the book Big Old Bones. Read the note at the end of the book also. Ask the students if they've ever heard of a dinosaur called a *thesaurus*. Hopefully, they're so deep into dinosaurs by now, that even if they have heard of the thesaurus, they'll be caught off guard and you'll really get their attention.

Show the transparency and tell the students that the thesaurus is not a kind of dinosaur, it's a dictionary of synonyms. Have the students define *synonym*. Show the students a thesaurus. Have the students recall another reference book that gives us information about words. Ask them to recall the information they can learn about a word in the dictionary (spelling, pronunciation, definition, part of speech, plural spelling, number of syllables, and, sometimes, use in a sentence). Explain that a thesaurus is similar to a dictionary because it tells about words and the entries are arranged in alphabetical order. The thesaurus, however, has a different purpose than the dictionary. A thesaurus can be used to find a variety of words that will make sentences in stories more interesting.

Look at the transparency again. Read the sentence next to the picture of the dinosaur. Ask the students if it's an interesting sentence. Tell them that they can find synonyms for many of the words which will make the sentence more descriptive. Distribute the thesauri, one to each table. Have the students find a synonym for *big* and write the new word in the blank of the four sentences beneath the dinosaur on the transparency. There may be some discussion about which of the synonyms to use. Have the students look up a synonym for *walked* and add it to the last three sentences. Find a synonym for *slowly* and add it to the last two sentences and, finally, find a synonym for *wet* for the last sentence. The last sentence may be something like: *The monstrous dinosaur trampled sluggishly through the soggy field.*

CLOSURE:
Remind the students that when they do descriptive writing they will want to use interesting words. Many times they'll be forced to think of synonyms on their own, but if possible they may get help from a thesaurus.

EXTENSION:
Distribute the paper and pencils. Show the students the poster. Have them write three simple sentences about what they see. Then have them go back and *elaborate*, using more descriptive words. They may use the thesaurus. Have a few of the students read their descriptions.

NOTES:
This lesson is actually an introduction to the thesaurus and is intended to introduce the reference book rather than to provide excessive practice in using it.

A THESAURUS IS NOT A DINOSAUR,
IT IS A BOOK OF SYNONYMS.

The big dinosaur walked slowly through the wet field.

The _____ dinosaur walked slowly through the wet field.

The _____ dinosaur _____ slowly through the wet field.

The _____ dinosaur _____ _____ through the wet field.

The _____ dinosaur _____ _____ through the _____ field.

GRADE 4	LIBRARY MEDIA INSTRUCTIONAL PLAN	DATE_____

Reference Bookmarks

LMC LEARNER STANDARDS

Orientation & Circulation
1. LMC Areas: REVIEW **Circulation Area; Fiction/Easy Section(s); Periodical Section; Reference Section; Nonfiction Section; Biography Section; Card/Computer Catalog**
2. Vocabulary: REVIEW **media; reference; fiction; nonfiction; periodicals; publisher; biography; atlas; almanac; call number; copyright date;** INTRODUCE **unabridged dictionary; thesaurus; verso**
3. REVIEW LMC Rules
4. REVIEW Local Circulation Procedures/ Check Out Books
5. REVIEW Book Care Rules

Literature Appreciation
1. Fiction
   01. Types: Historical, Realistic; Humorous; Adventure
   02. Elements: Character; Plot; Setting
2. Nonfiction
   01. Folklore (Fables, Folktales, Fairy Tales)
   02. Poetry
   03. Biography
   04. Informational
3. Multicultural Literature
4. Authors/Illustrators
5. Award Books (Newbery; Coretta Scott King)

Information Skills
1. Location of Materials: REVIEW / EXTEND Arrangement of Fiction Books; Arrangement of Nonfiction Books & Arrangement of Biography Books; INTRODUCE Arrangement of Audiovisual Materials
2. Parts of a Book: REVIEW **table of contents; title page; glossary, index;** INTRODUCE **dedication**
3. Research: REVIEW/EXTEND Alphabetical Order; Use of the Encyclopedia; Use of the Dictionary; Use of Periodicals; Use of Special Reference Books; INTRODUCE Use of Atlas; Use of Almanac; Children's Magazine Guide
4. Card/Computer Catalog: REVIEW /EXTEND Types of Cards/Searches & Card/Record Information

Technology
1. REVIEW/INTRODUCE Proper Use & Care of Appropriate AV Equipment & Software
2. REVIEW/INTRODUCE Viewing & Listening Skills

CURRICULUM CORRELATION

_____
_____
_____
_____
_____

MATERIALS:
Reference books from the Reference Section of the LMC
Pencils
Reference Bookmarks, Sample and Blank Bookmarks (see next pages)
Chalkboard and Chalk or Vocabulary Board

FOCUS:
Write the word *reference* on the chalkboard or find it on the vocabulary board. Ask students to find the root word *refer*. Have them define *refer* and look it up in the dictionary. One meaning is *to direct to a source for information*. Have students name some reference books they have used. ***Have the students locate the Reference Section of the LMC and tell them that we'll practice using some of the books there.***

ACTIVITY:
Display examples of the various kinds of reference books that are available in the LMC. Review the use of the index. Find the indices of several of the reference books and show that they are located in different parts of the various books.

Explain that it is necessary to remember important *Key Words* or *Catch Words* when doing research. Provide practice in determining the *Key Words* of several sample reference questions.

Remind students that it is important to never give up. If they don't find the answer on the first try, they should try again. Most of the fun in finding the answers to research questions is in the search itself.
ALWAYS KEEP LOOKING!

Divide the students into groups of two or three. Pass out the bookmarks, one to each student. Students in each group may work together to help each other answer the questions on their bookmarks.

CLOSURE:
After allowing students enough time to locate answers to a few questions, call the group back together. Students will share the answers to their questions and tell how they found them.

EXTENSION:
Some very capable students will find so much information during this LMC *scavenger hunt* that they will be interested in creating their own Reference Bookmarks. Some of the most challenging reference questions will be developed by students trying to *stump* other students.

For a greater challenge, do not include the source of the answer. The student will then need to determine which reference book to use.

Keep several bookmarks available for students to use at any time, or save some of the bookmarks and have Reference Contest in which students try to find the most answers during a week's time.

NOTES:
This lesson may last longer than one class session. It is also great for fifth and sixth grade classes. You might even give the sixth grade students some *blank* bookmarks and have them find questions for the fourth graders.

Webster's Biographical Dictionary

Beatrix Potter was the author of the little Peter Rabbit books. What was her first name?

World Book Encyclopedia ?

Test pilots fly new aircraft to check for safety. Name the two types of test pilots.

Bartlett's Familiar Quotations ?

What did Will Rogers say about the Mayflower?

Guinness Book of World Records ?

Name the man who was struck by lightning seven times and lived to tell about.

World Almanac ?

WHO INVENTED DYNAMITE ?

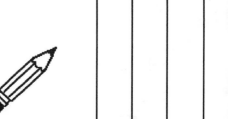

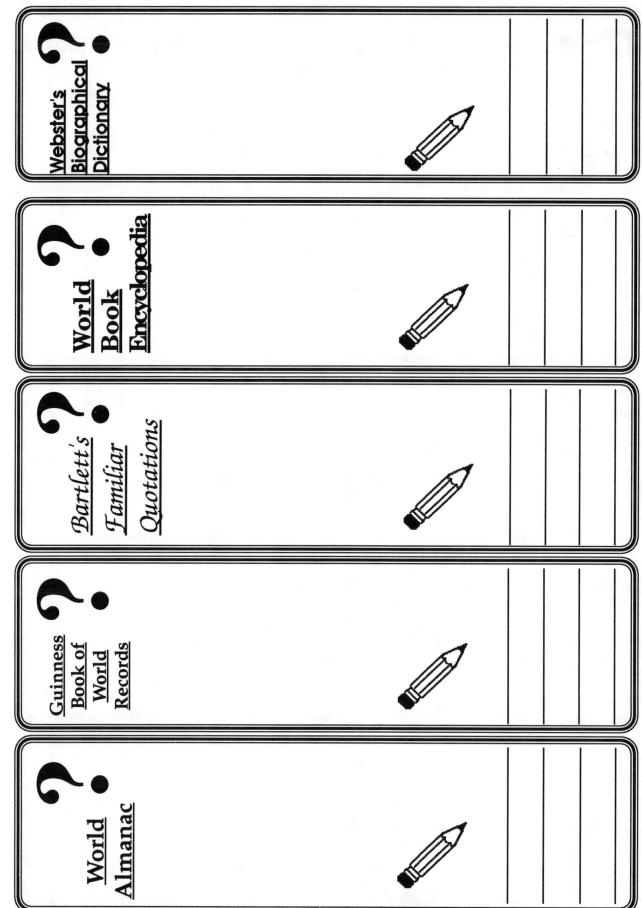

? ● Webster's Biographical Dictionary

? ● World Book Encyclopedia

? ● Bartlett's Familiar Quotations

? ● Guinness Book of World Records

? ● World Almanac

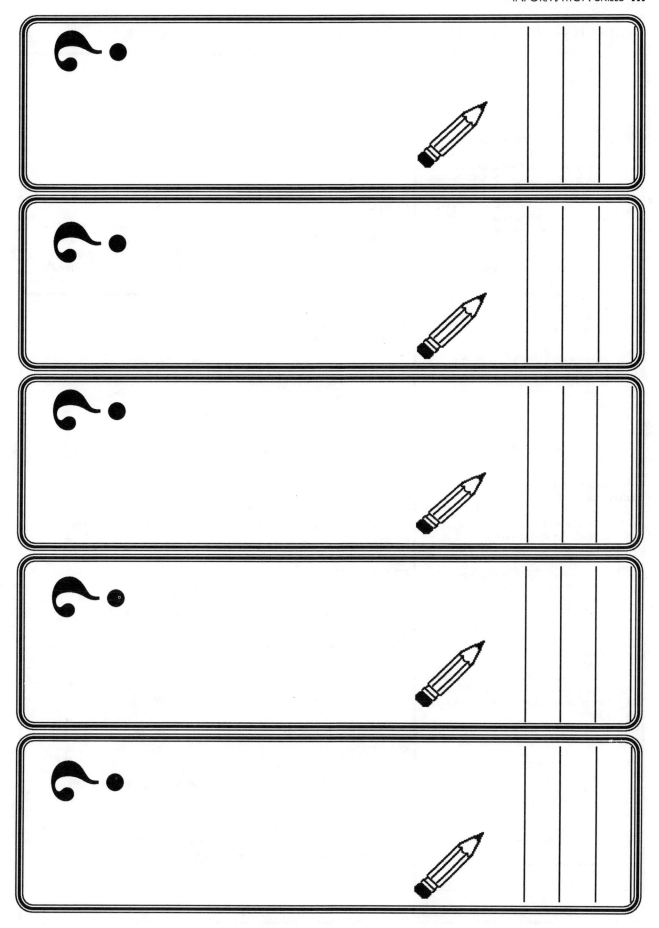

GRADE 5	LIBRARY MEDIA INSTRUCTIONAL PLAN	DATE_____

Dewey Posters

LMC LEARNER STANDARDS

Orientation & Circulation
1. LMC Areas: REVIEW **Circulation Area; Fiction/Easy Section(s); Periodical Section; Reference Section; Card/Computer Catalog; Biography Section; Nonfiction Section**
2. Vocabulary: REVIEW **media; reference; fiction; nonfiction; periodicals; publisher; biography; atlas; almanac;** INTRODUCE **audio; visual; classics**
3. REVIEW LMC Rules
4. REVIEW Local Circulation Procedures/ Check Out Books
5. REVIEW Book Care Rules

Literature Appreciation
1. Fiction
   01. Types: Science Fiction; Historical; Realistic
   02. Character; Plot; Setting; Theme
2. Nonfiction
   01. Folklore (Fables, Folktales, Fairy Tales; Tall Tales)
   02. Poetry
   03. Biography
   04. Informational
3. Multicultural Literature
4. Award Books (Newbery; Laura Ingalls Wilder)
5. Authors/Illustrators

Information Skills
1. Location of Materials: REVIEW/EXTEND Arrangement of Fiction Books; Arrangement of Nonfiction Books; Arrangement of Biography Books; Arrangement of AV Materials
2. Parts of a Book: INTRODUCE **preface & copyright page**
3. Research: REVIEW /EXTEND Use of Encyclopedia; Use of Dictionary; Use of Periodicals; Use of Special Reference Books; Use of Atlas; Use of Almanac; Children's Magazine Guide; INTRODUCE Use of Thesaurus
4. Card Catalog: REVIEW/EXTEND Types of Cards/Searches & Card/Record Information
5. Dewey Decimal System: INTRODUCE Ten Classes

Technology
1. REVIEW/INTRODUCE Proper Use & Care of Appropriate AV Equipment
2. REVIEW/INTRODUCE Viewing & Listening Skills

CURRICULUM CORRELATION

_____

_____

_____

_____

MATERIALS:
Poster listing the Ten Classes of the Dewey Decimal System
Chart Paper for Writing Student Responses
Discarded Magazines
Ten Sheets of Tagboard (24" x 18")
Glue
Markers
Scissors

FOCUS:
Remind students that books in the Nonfiction Section are arranged in numerical order and the system of arrangement is called the Dewey Decimal System. (Students must have already been introduced to the system in a previous lesson.) *Tell the students they will make posters illustrating the various topics found in each section of the Dewey Decimal System.*

ACTIVITY:
Discuss each of the ten Dewey classes with the students, having them give topics which would be included in each subject area.

As the students call out topics, write them on a large sheet of paper. Each list should be labeled with its Dewey Decimal Classification number at the top. Make sure the lists are accurate.

Divide the students into groups of three or four and give each group one of the lists describing a class of the Dewey Decimal System and a piece of tagboard. Have the students label their pieces of tagboard with the Dewey Classification number at the top.

The students can look through discarded magazines to find pictures which illustrate the topics on their lists. The pictures should be cut out and glued onto the tagboard to create a collage. Some pictures may need to be labeled to clarify the topic.

CLOSURE:
Have the students share their posters with the rest of the class. They should point out the various subjects found in their Dewey Classes.

EXTENSION:
Laminate the posters and hang them in the Library Media Center above the corresponding shelves of the Nonfiction Books Section.

NOTES:
This is not an introductory lesson. The students should have been previously introduced to the Dewey Decimal System, possibly through the use of a filmstrip or video, and should have some knowledge of the arrangement of the system.

This lesson will probably take more than one class session to complete. You may want to cover the 000s through the 400s in one session and the 500s through 900s in another. A separate poster may be made for the Biography Section.

GRADE 5	LIBRARY MEDIA INSTRUCTIONAL PLAN	DATE_____

Maps, Maps, Maps

LMC LEARNER STANDARDS

Orientation & Circulation
1. LMC Areas: REVIEW **Circulation Area; Fiction/Easy Section(s); Periodical Section; Reference Section; Nonfiction Section; Biography Section**
2. Vocabulary: REVIEW **media; reference; fiction; nonfiction; periodicals; publisher; biography; atlas; almanac; INTRODUCE audio; visual; classics**
3. REVIEW LMC Rules
4. REVIEW Local Circulation Procedures/ Check Out Books
5. REVIEW Book Care Rules

Literature Appreciation
1. Fiction
   01. Types: Science Fiction; Historical; Realistic
   02. Character; Plot; Setting; Theme
2. Nonfiction
   01. Folklore (Fables, Folktales, Fairy Tales; Tall Tales)
   02. Poetry
   03. Biography
   04. Informational
3. Multicultural Literature
4. Award Books (Newbery; Laura Ingalls Wilder)
5. Authors/Illustrators

Information Skills
1. Location of Materials: REVIEW/EXTEND Arrangement of Fiction Books; Arrangement of Nonfiction Books; Arrangement of Biography Books; Arrangement of AV Materials
2. Parts of a Book: INTRODUCE **preface & copyright page**
3. Research: REVIEW /EXTEND Use of Encyclopedia; Use of Dictionary; Use of Periodicals; Use of Special Reference Books; Use of Atlas; Use of Almanac; Children's Magazine Guide; INTRODUCE Use of Thesaurus
4. Card/Computer Catalog: REVIEW/EXTEND Types of Cards/Searches & Card Record Information
5. Dewey Decimal System: INTRODUCE Ten Classes

Technology
1. REVIEW/INTRODUCE Proper Use & Care of Appropriate AV Equipment
2. REVIEW/INTRODUCE Viewing & Listening Skills

CURRICULUM CORRELATION

Social Studies
_____
_____
_____
_____

MATERIALS:
Encyclopedias and Atlases
Paper and Pencils
Transparency Film (For an economical substitute, save large scraps of laminated film and cut them into 8 1/2" by 11" pieces.)
Overhead Projector, Transparency Pens
Wet and Dry Paper Towels

FOCUS:
Using a teacher-made or commercially-made transparency, show the students a map of their state indicating geographical features and major cities and towns. Point out the map key or legend. *Explain that the students will make transparencies of other states in the U.S. using encyclopedias and atlases.*

ACTIVITY:
Review with the students the process of locating a map in an atlas or an encyclopedia.

Assign each student a state and have him/her find a map of that state in the atlas or encyclopedia. (The students may work in pairs, if necessary.) Explain to the students that they are looking for physical/political maps that show both the geographical features and the major cities. They may want to include any other interesting landmarks. Remind them to include a map legend.

Provide the students with pencils and paper and the reference books. Have them do the map tracing with these first and then use the transparency film and transparency markers to trace from the paper. Using transparency markers with reference books is too risky. Remind the students to be very careful when using the markers near the books, especially when using damp paper towels for erasing and making corrections on the transparencies. Point out book care rules. Students should not press down hard with the pencil when tracing and should be careful not to make any marks in the atlases or encyclopedias.

CLOSURE:
When the transparencies are completed, the students can share them with the class. Explain the proper use and care of the overhead projector.

EXTENSION:
Each student can prepare a brief report about the state and use the transparency as a visual aid when presenting the report.

NOTES:
A variation of this lesson may be done using various maps of one state or a small map of the United States. Divide the students into groups. Make the following group assignments: Create a physical map only, identifying mountains, plains, rivers, valleys, lakes, etc. Create a map identifying the major cities and towns. Create a map identifying natural resources. Create a map identifying the major industries. Create a map showing major highways. The maps must all be drawn to the same scale. When they are all completed, the various maps can be overlaid showing correlation between industry, population, geography, etc.

This is an example of a cooperatively-planned activity integrating LMC skills into the curriculum. Two or three class sessions may be needed to complete this lesson.

GRADE 5	LIBRARY MEDIA INSTRUCTIONAL PLAN	DATE_____

Pocahontas

LMC LEARNER STANDARDS

Orientation & Circulation
1. LMC Areas: REVIEW **Circulation Area; Fiction/Easy Section(s); Periodical Section; Reference Section; Card/Computer Catalog; Nonfiction Section; Biography Section**
2. Vocabulary: REVIEW **media; reference; fiction; nonfiction; periodicals; publisher; biography; atlas; almanac;** INTRODUCE **audio; visual; classics**
3. REVIEW LMC Rules
4. REVIEW Local Circulation Procedures/ Check Out Books
5. REVIEW Book Care Rules

Literature Appreciation
1. Fiction
  01. Types: Science Fiction; Historical; Realistic
  02. Character; Plot; Setting; Theme
2. Nonfiction
  01. Folklore (Fables, Folktales, Fairy Tales; Tall Tales)
  02. Poetry
  03. Biography
  04. Informational
3. Multicultural Literature
4. Award Books (Newbery; Wilder)
5. Authors/Illustrators

Information Skills
1. Location of Materials: REVIEW/EXTEND Arrangement of Fiction Books; Arrangement of Nonfiction Books; Arrangement of Biography Books; Arrangement of AV Materials
2. Parts of a Book: INTRODUCE **preface & copyright page**
3. Research: REVIEW /EXTEND Use of Encyclopedia; Use of Dictionary; Use of Periodicals; Use of Special Reference Books; Use of Atlas; Use of Almanac; Children's Magazine Guide; INTRODUCE Use of Thesaurus
4. Card/Computer Catalog: REVIEW/EXTEND Types of Cards/Searches & Card/Record Information
5. Dewey Decimal System: INTRODUCE Ten Classes

Technology
1. REVIEW/INTRODUCE Proper Use & Care of Appropriate AV Equipment
2. REVIEW/INTRODUCE Viewing & Listening Skills

CURRICULUM CORRELATION
Social Studies

_____
_____
_____
_____
_____

MATERIALS:
Book, My Name Is Pocahontas by William Accorsi
Book, Double Life of Pocahontas by Jean Fritz
Map of the World, Overhead Projector, Transparency Pens
Transparency of "Pocahontas's Double Life" (see next page)
Groups Assignment Sheets of "Pocahontas's Double Life" (see next pages)
Notebook Paper, Pencils, Drawing Paper, Markers; Crayons, Tagboard, Glue
Various Reference and Nonfiction Books for Research

FOCUS:
Show the students the picture book, My Name Is Pocahontas and have them share any knowledge they have about Pocahontas. Identify her as an Indian girl who helped the first English settlers in the first permanent settlement in the New World. Ask them to identify the *New World*. Find Jamestown, Virginia on the map and identify it as the first permanent English settlement. ***Show the students the book* Double Life of Pocahontas *and tell them that we will investigate the life of Pocahontas and create a display depicting her double life.***

ACTIVITY:
Show the book Double Life of Pocahontas. Using the transparency, briefly discuss Pocahontas's *double life*. Find London, England on the map. Explain that November is Native American Heritage Month and there will be a display about Pocahontas, who was a Native American, although the land where she lived did not become *America* until many years after her death. Tell the students that they will be responsible for creating the display which will consist of Pocahontas standing near her homes in both Virginia and England with landscape scenes in the background.

Ask the students what sources they can use to complete this assignment (biography books about Pocahontas, encyclopedias, biographical dictionaries, nonfiction books about American History and English History, textbooks, and vertical file materials). Explain that there is not time to read everything about Pocahontas or American and English history, so they will need to find the exact information they'll need as quickly and directly as possible. Suggest that they use the card/computer catalog to find books. Ask what subjects they'll look up (*Pocahontas, Indians of North America, Jamestown, England -- History, U.S. -- History*). Ask what topics they might look up in the encyclopedia and in the indexes of the books they're using (*Powhatan*, Pocahontas' father and chief of the Indians living in the area, *Pocahontas, Jamestown, England*). Write these words on the transparency as reminders.

Divide the students into two groups. One group will work on the life of Pocahontas as an Indian and the other will work on her life as an English woman. They will need to make a *paper figure* of Pocahontas, dressed appropriately, a large poster showing landscape for *background* and a separate drawing or model of a *house* like the one Pocahontas may have lived in. They may add other figures (Powhatan, John Smith, John Rolfe or Thomas, her baby) if they'd like. Give each group a Group Assignment Sheet. Have them complete the sheet in one or two class sessions and build the displays in another two sessions.

CLOSURE:
When the displays are ready, make a timeline of Pocahontas's life to display also. Use the display of the life of Pocahontas as an Indian during the first two weeks of November and the one of her life as an English woman during the second two weeks.

EXTENSION:
A student may have an Indian doll that could be dressed appropriately and used in the display instead of the drawing of Pocahontas.

NOTES:
You may want to have more than one class of fifth grade students work on this project. One class could work on the *Indian* part and another on the *English* part.

Life of Pocahontas as...

an Indian Princess   &   **an English Lady**

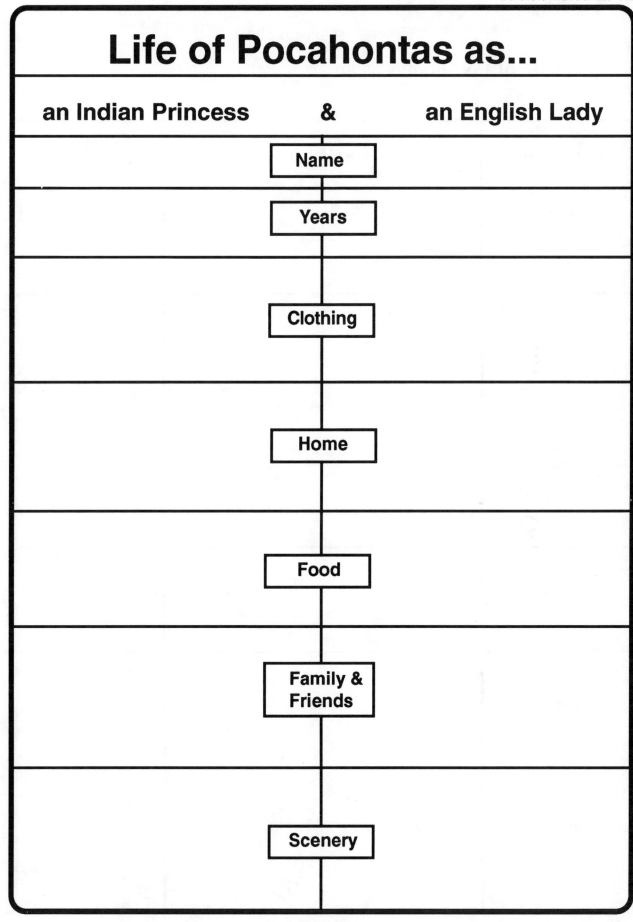

Name

Years

Clothing

Home

Food

Family & Friends

Scenery

Group Assignment Sheet

Life of Pocahontas as an _____

Assignment	Description	Students Responsible
Pocahontas Figure		
House		
Background Scenery		
Other Figures		
Props		
Written Description		

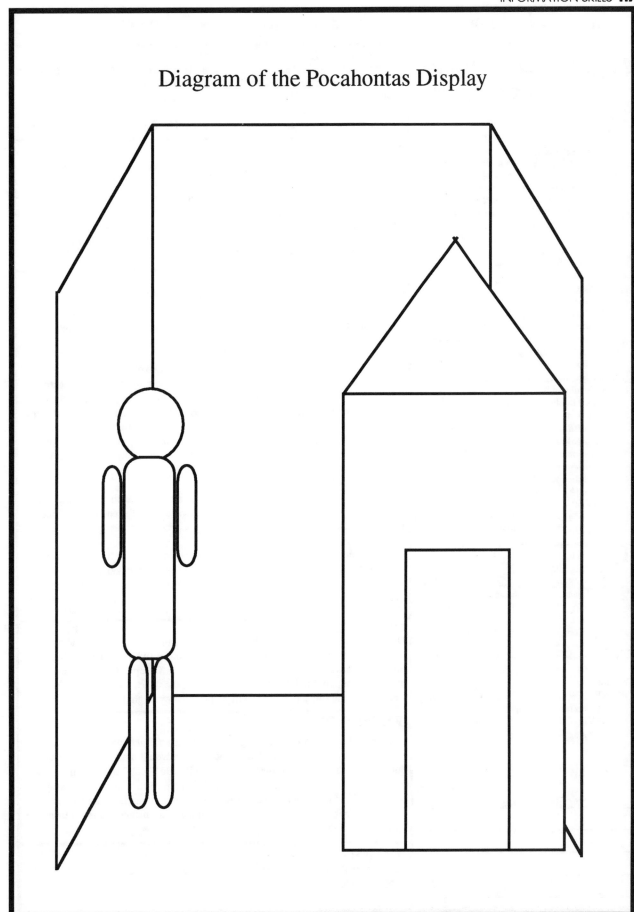

Diagram of the Pocahontas Display

GRADE 6	LIBRARY MEDIA INSTRUCTIONAL PLAN	DATE_____

Biographical Dictionary

LMC LEARNER STANDARDS
Orientation & Circulation
1. LMC Areas: REVIEW **Circulation Area;
   Fiction/Easy Section(s); Periodical Section;
   Reference Section; Card/Computer Catalog;
   Nonfiction Section** Biography Section
2. Vocabulary REVIEW **media; fiction;
   reference; nonfiction; periodicals;
   publisher; biography; atlas; audio; visual;
   classics;** INTRODUCE **autobiography**
3. REVIEW LMC Rules
4. REVIEW Local Circulation Procedures/
   Check Out Books
5. REVIEW Book Care Rules

Literature Appreciation
1. Fiction
   01. All Types
   02. Character; Plot; Setting; Theme; Style
2. Nonfiction
   01. Folklore (Fables, Folktales, Fairy Tales;
   Tall Tales; Mythology & Legends)
   02. Poetry
   03. Biography/Autobiography
3. Multicultural Literature
4. Award Books (Newbery; Carnegie; Coretta
   Scott King)
5. Authors/Illustrators

Information Skills
1. Location of Materials: REVIEW/EXTEND
   Arrangement of Fiction Books; Arrangement
   of Nonfiction Books; Arrangement of
   Biography Books & Arrangement of AV
   Materials
2. Parts of a Book: REVIEW **preface; copyright
   page;** INTRODUCE **bibliography; footnotes;
   preface; appendices**
3. Research: REVIEW /EXTEND Use of
   Encyclopedia; Use of Periodicals; Use of
   Special Reference Books; Use of Atlas ; Use
   of Almanac; Use of Thesaurus; Children's
   Magazine Guide; REINFORCE Outlining for
   Research
4. Card/Computer Catalog: REVIEW Types of
   Cards/Searches & Card/Record Information
5. Dewey Decimal System: REVIEW / EXTEND
   Ten Classes & Recognize Subject of Each

Technology
1. REVIEW/INTRODUCE Proper Use & Care of
   Appropriate AV Equipment
2. REVIEW/INTRODUCE Viewing &
   Listening Skills

CURRICULUM CORRELATION

Social Studies

MATERIALS:
Reference Books, <u>Webster's Biographical Dictionary</u>, <u>Who's Who in Black America</u>, <u>Dictionary of American Biography</u>, and <u>Who's Who in Hispanic America</u>
Transparency, "Biographical Dictionaries Comparison Chart" (see next page)
For Extension Project:
Student Profile Sheets (see next pages); Student Photos; Pens; Binder; Hole Punch

FOCUS:
Ask students to define *biography* and have them point out the location of the biography books in the LMC. Ask them if they can think of another place in the LMC where they could find information about the lives of famous people (encyclopedias). Point out the location of the encyclopedias in the Reference Section of the LMC. Show the students the <u>Webster's Biographical Dictionary</u>. *Explain that there are other reference books in addition to the encyclopedias that offer information about people and we will compare several of those sources.*

ACTIVITY:
Tell the students that we'll compare the information about a person found in a biography book, an encyclopedia and a biographical dictionary. Have one student find a biography about Abraham Lincoln and have another student find an encyclopedia entry about Lincoln.

Look up *Lincoln* in <u>Webster's Biographical Dictionary</u>, explaining that the entries are in alphabetical order by the subject's last name. Show the students the entry for Lincoln. Have them look at the biography book and the encyclopedia article and compare them in length to the entry in the biographical dictionary. Ask the students which of the three resources they would need to use to write a detailed report about Lincoln. They could start with the encyclopedia, but they may need more information from the book. Iif they just needed an outline of Lincoln's life, they might try the biographical dictionary.

Ask the students what kind of information about a person they might find in a biographical dictionary. After their responses, read them the entry about Lincoln. Point out that only the important details about a person's life are given.

Have the students name a president or ex-president who is still living and look him up in the biographical dictionary. Explain that he's not included because he is still living and only people of the past are included in <u>Webster's Biographical Dictionary</u>. Show the students the introduction of the book that explains who can and cannot be included.

CLOSURE:
Divide the students into three groups and give each group one of the other biographical dictionaries. Have them read the introductions to find out who is included in each one. Show the transparency, "Biographical Dictionaries Comparison Chart" and have each group supply the information to complete the chart. As you examine each source, have the students try to identify a person they might find in each one.

EXTENSION:
Tell the students that we are making our own biographical dictionary called <u>Who's Who in Our School</u>. To be included, each person would have been at *our school* during the sixth grade. Distribute the "Student Profile Sheets" and help the students complete them. Ask each student to bring a photograph from home or take a snapshot of each student for the book. When the profile sheets are completed, hole-punch each one, put them in alphabetical order by the students' last names and insert them in a binder labeled with the title.

NOTES:
This project can be updated each year. Reference sources will vary according to the LMC collection.

BIOGRAPHICAL DICTIONARIES COMPARISON CHART

Title	Criteria to Be Included	Information Listed

Who's Who at _____

Last Name, First Name, Middle Initial

Birthday

Parents

Brothers & Sisters

Teacher/Class _____

Date _____

Schools Attended

_____

_____

Honors & Awards

_____

_____

Clubs & Organizations

_____

_____

Goals & Ambitions

_____

_____

Who's Who at _____

Last Name, First Name, Middle Initial

Birthday

Parents

Brothers & Sisters

Clubs & Organizations

Goals & Ambitions

Schools Attended

Honors & Awards

Teacher/Class _____

Date _____

GRADE 6	LIBRARY MEDIA INSTRUCTIONAL PLAN	DATE_____

Touring with Dewey

LMC LEARNER STANDARDS

Orientation & Circulation
1. LMC Areas: REVIEW **Circulation Area; Fiction/Easy Section(s); Reference Section; Card/Computer Catalog; Periodical Section; Nonfiction Section; Biography Section**
2. Vocabulary REVIEW **media; fiction; reference; nonfiction; periodicals; publisher; biography; atlas; audio; visual; classics;** INTRODUCE **autobiography**
3. REVIEW LMC Rules
4. REVIEW Local Circulation Procedures/ Check Out Books
5. REVIEW Book Care Rules

Literature Appreciation
1. Fiction
   01. All Types
   02. Character; Plot; Setting; Theme; Style
2. Nonfiction
   01. Folklore (Fables; Folktales; Fairy Tales; Tall Tales; Mythology & Legends)
   02. Poetry
   03. Biography/Autobiography
3. Multicultural Literature
4. Award Books (Newbery; Carnegie; Coretta Scott King)
5. Authors/Illustrators

Information Skills
1. Location of Materials: REVIEW/EXTEND Arrangement of Fiction Books; Arrangement of Nonfiction Books; Arrangement of Biography Books & Arrangement of AV Materials
2. Parts of a Book: REVIEW **preface; copyright page;** INTRODUCE **bibliography; footnotes; preface; appendices**
3. Research: REVIEW/EXTEND Use of Encyclopedia; Use of Periodicals; Use of Special Reference Books; Use of Atlas ; Use of Almanac; Use of Thesaurus; Children's Magazine Guide; REINFORCE Outlining for Research
4. Card/Computer Catalog: REVIEW Types of Cards/Searches & Card/Record Information
5. Dewey Decimal System: REVIEW/EXTEND Ten Classes & Recognize Subject of Each

Technology
1. REVIEW/INTRODUCE Proper Use & Care of Appropriate Audiovisual Equipment
2. REVIEW/INTRODUCE Viewing & Listening Skills

CURRICULUM CORRELATION

Social Studies

_____

_____

_____

_____

MATERIALS:
World map or atlas
Filmstrip, The Funny Little Woman by Blair Lent (Folktale, 300s)
Book, Cooking the Japanese Way by Reiko Weston (Technology, 600s)
Book, Origami, Japanese Paper Folding by Florence Sakade (Fine Arts, 700s)
Book, Red Dragonfly on My Shoulder by S. Cassedy (Literature, 800s)
Book, Count Your Way Through Japan by Jim Haskins (History, 900s)
Chart of the 900 Class of the Dewey Decimal System
Origami Paper

FOCUS:
Have a student find the country of Japan on a map of the world or in an atlas of the world. Ask students where in the LMC we could find information about Japan. (They may know to look in the 900s for history and geography books.) *Explain that we will use the Dewey Decimal System to help us look at the Japanese culture.*

ACTIVITY:
Introduce and show the filmstrip The Funny Little Woman. Explain that it is a Caldecott Medal book and that it is also a Japanese folktale. Ask students to name the Dewey Decimal class for folktales (300s).

Go to the 600 shelves of the Nonfiction Section and identify it as Applied Science or Technology. Ask students to think of the kinds of books that might be found on these shelves. Find the cookbooks and select the book Cooking the Japanese Way. Have a student read one of the recipes

Using a piece of origami paper, demonstrate paper folding. Have students identify what you are doing. Most of them will know about origami. Ask students where they would find books about Oriental art and go to the 700 shelves to find one.

Have students recall what kinds of books are found in the 800s. Ask them if they can identify a kind of Japanese poetry called *haiku*. Go to the shelves and get a book of haiku. Have a couple of volunteers read two or three of the poems. Identify *haiku* as short nature poems with a total of 17 syllables.

Finally, go to the 900 shelves which contain history and geography books. Show the students a chart of the Dewey divisions of the 900 class. Have them find the classification numbers for Japanese geography (915.2) and Japanese history (952). Find several sample books and share the contents with the class.

CLOSURE:
Have students review the classes of the Dewey Decimal System that have been discussed during the lesson and have them identify the various books about Japan which were found in each Dewey class.

EXTENSION:
There are a variety of projects: Act out a Japanese folktale.
Write haiku poems.
Make origami animals.
Cook a Japanese dish or arrange a visit from a chef of a local Japanese restaurant.

NOTES:
Books used in this lesson may vary according to individual LMC collections, but these are recommended titles. A great book for the classroom teacher to read aloud during this lesson is Sadako and the Thousand Paper Cranes by Eleanor Coerr. *This lesson could be done using a variety of other countries.*

GRADE 6	LIBRARY MEDIA INSTRUCTIONAL PLAN	DATE_____

Tic Tac Toe

LMC LEARNER STANDARDS
Orientation & Circulation
1. LMC Areas; REVIEW **Nonfiction Section; Fiction/Easy Section(s); Reference Section; Periodical Section; Card/Computer Catalog; Circulation Area; Reference Section; Biography Section**
2. Vocabulary REVIEW **media; fiction; reference; nonfiction; periodicals; publisher; biography; atlas; audio; visual; classics;** INTRODUCE **autobiography**
3. REVIEW LMC Rules
4. REVIEW Local Circulation Procedures/ Check Out Books
5. REVIEW Book Care Rules

Literature Appreciation
1. Fiction
   01. All Types
   02. Character; Plot; Setting; Theme; Style
2. Nonfiction
   01. Folklore (Fables, Folktales, Fairy Tales; Tall Tales; Mythology & Legends)
   02. Poetry
   03. Biography/Autobiography
3. Multicultural Literature
4. Award Books (Newbery; Carnegie; Coretta Scott King)
5. Authors/Illustrators

Information Skills
1. Location of Materials: REVIEW/EXTEND Arrangement of Fiction Books; Arrangement of Nonfiction Books; Arrangement of Biography Books & Arrangement of AV Materials
2. Parts of a Book: REVIEW **preface; copyright page;** INTRODUCE **bibliography; footnotes; preface; appendices**
3. Research: REVIEW/EXTEND Use of Encyclopedia; Use of Periodicals; Use of Special Reference Books; Use of Atlas ; Use of Almanac; Use of Thesaurus; Children's Magazine Guide; REINFORCE Outlining for Research
4. Card/Computer Catalog: REVIEW Types of Cards/Searches & Card/Record Information
5. Dewey Decimal System: REVIEW/EXTEND Ten Classes & Recognize Subject of Each

Technology
1. REVIEW/INTRODUCE Proper Use & Care of Appropriate Audiovisual Equipment
2. REVIEW/INTRODUCE Viewing & Listening Skills

CURRICULUM CORRELATION
_____
_____
_____
_____
_____

MATERIALS:
25 - 30 3" x 5" Question Cards (The questions must be written in advance of the game and can come from all areas of the Learner Standards or can concentrate on one area that is being taught at the time.) (See next page)
Chalk and Chalkboard or Overhead Transparency, Overhead Projector and Transparency Pens
Two Drinking Straws, One Long and One Short (Optional)

FOCUS:
Ask students to recall some game shows they've seen on television. Ask them if they remember one that's like the game Tic Tac Toe. Tell them that we'll pay a game similar to that today, but all the questions will be about the Library Media Center. *Tell the students that we'll review all of their Information Skills.*

ACTIVITY:
Draw a large Tic Tac Toe grid on the chalkboard.
Divide the students into two teams and have them line up, one behind the other.
Name one team *X's* and the other team *O's* and write the two names on the chalkboard.

There are two ways to play the game:

Give a piece of chalk to the first student in each line.
Read a question and let the first of those two students who raises his/her hand try to answer the question. If the question is answered incorrectly, the student on the other team gets a chance. If both of those students miss the question, let any students from either team, who raises his hand first, try to answer the question. The team who finally gets the correct answer will mark the *X* or *O* on the Tic Tac Toe grid.
Pass the chalk back to the next person in line and repeat the process

Here is another method of play:

Have two students, one from each team, *draw straws* to see which team will go first. Ask the first question to the first player on team one. If the answer is correct, that students places the *X* or *O* on the Tic Tac Toe grid. (The chalk is kept at the chalkboard.) If that student misses the question, the first student on team two gets a chance and the question is asked back and forth between the two teams until a student can answer it. The students keep their places in line; they do not move to the back after a question.

The following rules apply to both methods of play:
The first team to get *three in a row* wins the game.
If any students yells out the answer, the other team gets a *free turn* to answer the question.
Keep a tally of the number of games won by each team. At the end of the class, the team that has won the most games is declared the winner.

CLOSURE:
As the students play the game, make a mental note of the questions that give them the most trouble. Before the students leave, review those questions.

EXTENSION:
Have the students give ideas for questions to be added to the cards.

NOTES:
Include some easy and difficult questions to give *slower* students a chance at success. Shuffle the cards occasionally so that questions will be repeated.

Sample Questions for Tic Tac Toe

What does the term **circulation** mean in the LMC?

Define **media**.

What is **folklore**?

What is a **fiction** book?

What is the subject of books found in 900 section of the nonfiction books?

Name two types of reference books.

Where in the call number located on a catalog card?

Define **card catalog**.

What is the arrangement of fiction books.

Define **biography**.

Define **author**.

What does an **illustrator** do?

Name two rules of book care.

What is the **Newbery Medal**?

What is the job of the publisher of a book?

Name three things found on the title page of a book.

Define **table of contents**.

Name three things you can find out about a word by looking in a dictionary.

When would you use an almanac?

When would you use a periodical?

Define **periodical?**

Describe the process used to borrow a book from the LMC.

Name one author that has received the Newbery Medal.

Define **encyclopedia.**

Define **biographical dictionary**.

What is the difference between an **autobiography** and a **biography**?

What is the **Kate Greenaway Medal**?

What is the **Caldecott Medal**?

Are folktales shelved in the fiction or the nonfiction section of the LMC?

What country awards the **Carnegie Medal**?

Define **atlas**.

When would you use an atlas?

Define **bibliography**.

How is an index arranged in the back of a book?

Define **audiovisual**.

What information is found in the preface of a book?

Name three types of cards found in the card catalog.

What section of the Dewey Decimal System contains poetry books?

Where would you find sports books in the Dewey Decimal System?

What kind of books would you find in the 500 section of the nonfiction books?

How are nonfiction books arranged on the LMC shelves.

What kind of books are awarded the **Coretta Scott King Award**?

Define **copyright date.**

Name three types of **folklore**.

RESOURCES

Accorsi, Michael. *My Name Is Pocahontas*. New York: Holiday House, 1992. The life of the Indian princess who figured so prominently in history, is retold in a picture book format.

Aliki. *Digging Up Dinosaurs*. New York: Crowell, 1981. The process of finding dinosaur bones and putting them together as skeletons is discussed.

———. *Dinosaur Bones*. New York: Crowell, 1988. Scientists can discover much about prehistoric days by studying the fossils of dinosaurs.

———. *Dinosaurs Are Different*. New York: Crowell, 1985. The author describes various types of dinosaurs and their differences.

———. *Fossils Tell of Long Ago*. New York: Crowell, 1972. The process of finding and reconstructing fossilized bones is presented in simple text and illustrations by the author.

———. *My Visit to the Dinosaurs*. New York: Crowell, 1969, 1985. A young boy's visit to the museum of natural history teaches him about various kinds of dinosaurs.

Anderson, Hans Christian. *Ugly Duckling* New York: Scribner, 1985. The classic tale of the *duckling* that grew up to be a swan.

Carrick, Carol. *Big Old Bones*. New York: Clarion, 1989. An eccentric professor finds a bunch of dinosaur bones and puts them together to create some interesting creatures.

Cohen, Miriam. *Don't Eat Too Much Turkey*. New York: Greenwillow Books, 1987. Jim and his friends in the first grade celebrate the Thanksgiving holidays in their own individual ways.

———. *When Will I Read?* Boston: Greenwillow, 1977. First grader, Jim, is very anxious to learn to read.

Demi. *In the Eyes of the Cat*. New York: Henry Holt, 1992. The artist interprets several Japanese poems through beautiful detailed pictures.

Flack, Marjorie. *Angus and the Ducks*. New York: Doubleday, 1931. A Scottie dog plays with some pesky ducks.

————. *Story about Ping*. New York: Viking Press, 1933. A duckling, living on the Yangtze River in China, wanders away in search of adventure.

Freeman, Don. *Corduroy*. New York: Viking Press, 1968. A little bear who lives in a department store looks for his missing button so someone will buy him and take him home.

Fritz, Jean. *Double Life of Pocahontas*. New York: Putnam, 1983. The author has written a concise and accurate account of the Indian princess, about whom so many stories have been told.

Ginsburg, Mirra. *Chick and the Duckling*. New York: Macmillan Publishing Company, 1972. A chick and a duckling hatch from their eggs at the same time and the chick wants to do everything the duck does—except swim.

Goldin, Augusta. *Ducks Don't Get Wet*. New York: Crowell, 1989. The author presents facts about the lives of ducks, including the reason they don't get wet when they swim.

Haskins, Jim. *Count Your Way through Japan*. Minneapolis: Carolrhoda, 1987. The reader learns to count in Japanese and also discovers many facts about the country of Japan.

Isenhart, Hans-Heinrich. *A Duckling Is Born*. New York: Putnam, 1981. Colorful photographs trace the life of a Mallard duck, showing his growth inside the egg, his birth and first swim.

Kennedy, Jimmy. *The Teddy Bears' Picnic*. Old Tappan: Green Tiger Press, 1983. A book and accompanying record describing the day when all the teddy bears gather in the woods to have a picnic.

Kroll, Stephen. *Oh What a Thanksgiving*. New York: Scholastic, Inc., 1988. A young boy celebrating his own Thanksgiving feast imagines what the first occasion might have been like.

Kraus, Robert. *Owliver* New York: Simon and Schuster, 1979, 1984. A little owl can't decide what to be when he grows up—a playwright for his mother or a doctor for his father—so he follows his heart.

Martin, Bill, Jr. *Brown Bear, Brown Bear, What Do You See?* New York: Henry Holt and Company, 1967. The author uses simple text and common animals to introduce children to colors.

McCloskey, Robert. *Make Way for Ducklings*. New York: VikingPress, 1941, 1969. A family of ducks decide to settle in Boston's Public Gardens.

Mosel, Arlene. *The Funny Little Woman*. New York: Dutton, 1972. The author retells a wonderful Japanese folk tale about a little boy whose name was so long, he almost drowned before his younger brother could tell someone that the boy was in the well.

Petty, Kate. *Ducklings*. New York: Gloucester Press, 1990. The life of a duckling is shown through simple text and photographs.

Sakade, Florence. *Origami, Japanese Paper Folding*. Boston: Charles E. Tuttle, 1957. The author gives step-by-step instructions for making a variety of objects using the Japanese art of paper folding.

Selsam, Millicent. *A First Look at Ducks, Geese and Swans*. New York: Walker and Company, 1990. Simple text and illustrations describe these three types of water birds.

Sendak, Maurice. *Where the Wild Things Are*. New York: Harper Collins, 1963. Max gets in trouble for acting *wild* and is sent to his room where he has a great imaginary adventure.

Tafuri, Nancy. *Have You Seen My Duckling?* New York: Greenwillow, 1984. A duckling is hidden among the delicate, stylized drawings on each page of this book.

Weston, Reiko. *Cooking the Japanese Way*. Minneapolis: Lerner Publications, 1983. This cookbook contains recipes for several Japanese dishes and includes some information about the country of Japan, as well.

Wildsmith, Brian. *Little Wood Duck*. New York: Watts, 1973. The youngest in a family of wood ducks is taunted because he swims in a circle instead of a line with his brothers and sisters.

5 TECHNOLOGY

For at least the past ten years, there have been dire predictions of the demise of the book as we know it, with pages of paper and a cover of cloth. These prophesies were made, of course, based on the sudden advances in technology that occurred with the development of the microcomputer chip. According to these predictions, every family today should own a computer and should be sharing and receiving all necessary information via a modem connected to a computer in the local public library. Although that technology is developing, its progress is much slower than originally predicted. Even then, most technological advances take years to trickle down to the elementary school library media centers.

Even in the modern library media center books are still the most common sources of information. Nevertheless, audiovisual materials such as audiocassettes and filmstrips have been in use for many years in school classrooms as instructional aids, and in this area school library media centers have advanced more quickly than public libraries. Computer technology was slower in coming to the school library media centers, probably because it is difficult to look at computer software as simply another kind of media. Today, computers are fairly commonplace, even in school library media centers. Many circulation systems are computerized and more and more card catalogs are being replaced by the computerized catalog.

The responsibility for instruction in the use of audiovisual material and the hardware associated with it usually belongs to the library media specialist in the school. Unfortunately, in some situations, the LMS must instruct the students in keyboarding and other computer skills. This type of in-depth instruction can only diminish the overall library media program and is quite different from teaching students to use the computer for seeking information.

Two general learner standards are appropriate for each grade level in the area of technology. The first standard involves teaching the proper care and use of audiovisual material. The library media specialist does not teach a separate lesson on this topic. Instead, use and care of equipment, including computers, is taught as the LMS is using audiovisual materials in the course of presenting a lesson on any given topic. For instance, as the LMS is showing a videotaped program about using reference books, he or she should point out that students should never open the flap on the front of the videocassette to touch the magnetic tape inside and should store the videotape in its plastic cover to protect it from dust.

The second learner standard deals with viewing and listening skills which are important even if audiovisual materials are not being used in the lesson. There is a definite progression of these skills and again, the LMS should make sure the students use these skills when audiovisual materials are used in any lesson. In the following list of viewing and listening skills, the first two are introduced in kindergarten and another skill is added for each grade level. Remember, the skills are cumulative and by the time the student is in the sixth grade, the LMS should be employing all of them.

Viewing and Listening Skills:

1. Focus attention on AV presentation
2. Recall details from AV presentation
3. Participate in discussion following AV presentation
4. Paraphrase information from AV presentation
5. Understand and interpret information from AV presentation
6. Realize that information is available in a variety of formats
7. Use critical thinking skills to evaluate content of AV presentations
8. Use a variety of media for gathering and using information

Because these skills are not taught in isolated lessons, this chapter does not include any instructional plans for the area of technology. If audiovisual materials are used in the lessons in the other chapters, those learner standards are included as part of the lesson. This chapter instead includes descriptions of audiovisual programs which can be used in teaching information skills. Several formats are included—sound filmstrips, videotapes and computer programs. The availability and ease of use of videotaped programs has revolutionized the audiovisual industries. Many filmstrips are being transferred to videotape and other filmstrip programs are being discontinued. The filmstrip is still the most useful format for teaching library media skills. The projected picture is larger than that of a television screen and the students are not as mesmerized by the projected image as they are when they sit in front of a television screen. In addition, the library media specialist can more easily pause the filmstrip for discussion. Video programs that use live action can, of course, be very appealing and if the action enhances the subject being taught, these programs are useful. A few library media specialists have been caught up in the video revolution and are no longer buying filmstrips. In the selection of audiovisual programs, always consider the use of the material and the audience that will use it. Ease of use is certainly not the most important factor in selection.

The materials included on the following list constitute only a fraction of what is available, but they were selected because they have been used successfully with students. The list does not include materials that are used as actual sources of information by students and teachers, such as computerized reference sources. Instead, it includes materials that explain how to use reference sources. Other programs not included are those which present children's books in other formats such as filmstrips, audiocassettes, and videocassettes. While several of these have been used in the lessons presented in this book, they are not so much instructional materials as they are alternate formats of literary works. Many of these programs are available from several producers and are highly recommended for sharing literature with children.

A final note must be included in any chapter on using audiovisual materials. While these materials are great for introducing and summarizing lessons in any subject area, audiovisual programs must be introduced to the students as well. The students must be prepared for viewing the program by giving them any necessary background information and introducing any unfamiliar vocabulary used in the program. Above all, the LMS should watch, listen to, or use the audiovisual program with the children when teaching the lesson. If the LMS does not participate in the viewing of the program, the students will get the message that the information being presented is not really important.

The audiovisual materials listed here are arranged according to their vendors.

- Pied Piper/AIMS Media
- Eye Gate Media
- Society for Visual Education
- Cheshire Company

- Great Plains National/PBS
- R. R. Bowker
- Library Filmstrip Center
- American School Publisher/SRA
- Weston Woods

TITLE: *Literature for Children, Series 1*   **FORMAT:** 4 Sound Filmstrips or 2 VHS Videotapes
(Videotapes are Filmstrip to Video Transfers)

CONTENTS:

"Fantasy"   Students are introduced to several well-known books of fantasy and their authors and the arrangement of fiction books in the Library Media Center is discussed.

"Tall Tales"   Several tall tale heroes are discussed and students are introduced to the Nonfiction Section of the Library Media Center.

"Story of a Book"   The students meet the author, Holling C. Holling and discover the process of writing a book.

"Biography"   The meaning of *biography* is discussed through the book Benjamin Franklin by Ingri and Edgar D'Aulaire. The arrangement and location of the biography section of the Library Media Center is also discussed.

Teacher Guides Included

NOTES:

These programs work perfectly for introducing the parts of the LMC and the various kinds of books located in each section to students in the third and fourth grades. They can also be used for review with fifth and sixth grades. With adequate preparation, these programs can also be used with second grade toward the end of the school year.

PRODUCER: Pied Piper/AIMS Media   **PRICE:**   Filmstrips, $120.00
9710 DeSoto Avenue   Videotapes, $125.00
Chatsworth, CA 91311-4409

TITLE: *Literature for Children, Series 2*   **FORMAT:** 4 Sound Filmstrips or 2 VHS Videotapes
(Videotapes are Filmstrip to Video Transfers)

CONTENTS:

"Animals"   The differences between fiction and nonfiction are discussed through the use of Marguerite Henry's King of the Wind.

"Distant Lands"   The use of books to discover other lands is presented along with the use of reference books.

"Fairy Tales"   The origins and appeal of fairy tales and folk tales are discussed through depictions of Hansel and Gretel and Issun Boshi, the Inchling.

"Humor"   The humor found in children's stories is demonstrated through Mr. Popper's Penguins and Ribsy.

Teacher Guides included

NOTES:

Although this series of programs was produced several years ago, the producers had enough foresight to use literature which has lasting appeal and quality. These programs are excellent for introducing third and fourth grade students to a variety of types of fiction books.

PRODUCER: Pied Piper/AIMS Media   **PRICE:**   Filmstrips, $120.00
9710 DeSoto Avenue   Videotapes, $125.00
Chatsworth, CA 91311-4409

TITLE: *Literature for Children, Series 3*   **FORMAT:** 4 Sound Filmstrips or 2 VHS Videotapes
(Videotapes are Filmstrip to Video Transfers)

CONTENTS:

"Enjoying Illustration"   The pictures of forty illustrators are presented and discussed.

"Historical Fiction"   Works of fiction which are based on historical fact are discussed through the introduction of The Perilous Road and Island of the Blue Dolphins. The importance of accurate research and the use of author cards in the card catalog are also covered.

"Myths"   Mythology is discussed through the introduction of three mythological characters: King Midas, Pandora and Ulysses.

"Adventure"   The elements of fiction are discussed from the perspective of the adventure story Call It Courage. In addition, the use of title cards in the card catalog is included.

Teacher Guides Included

NOTES:

These programs are great introductions to several outstanding works of literature in several genres. The use of the card catalog is mentioned as a natural part of the script and demonstrates its use as a *means to an end* rather than *an end in itself*. The computerized catalog is not mentioned, but the similarities could be pointed out by the LMS.

PRODUCER: Pied Piper/AIMS Media   **PRICE:**   Filmstrips, $120.00
9710 DeSoto Avenue   Videotapes, $125.00
Chatsworth, CA 91311-4409

TITLE: *Literature for Children, Series 4*   **FORMAT:** 4 Sound Filmstrips or 2 VHS Videotapes
(Videotapes are Filmstrip to Video Transfers)

CONTENTS:

"Haiku" Using beautiful slides of nature outdoors, this filmstrip clearly depicts the inspiration for this Japanese form of poetry. The filmstrip sets the mood so that students are ready to write some of their own haiku poetry after viewing it.

"Descriptive Words" The filmstrip reminds the students that poetry is a rhythmic, verbal, descriptive interpretation of everything they see around them.

"Sounds of Poetry" Everyday sounds can inspire poetry in this filmstrip which stresses the rhythmic movement of verse.

"Humorous Verse" Poems are made humorous by the use of exaggeration, nonsense and the element of surprise.

Teacher Guides Included

NOTES:

Children love poetry and they want to write poems of their own. Two obstacles stand in the way: finding a rhythm that doesn't necessarily have to rhyme and finding that inspiration and motivation. This set of filmstrips will help the students overcome those obstacles and learn to write *from the heart.*

PRODUCER: Pied Piper/AIMS Media   **PRICE:** Filmstrips, $120.00
9710 DeSoto Avenue   Videotapes, $125.00
Chatsworth, CA 91311-4409

TITLE: *Literature for Children, Series 5*   **FORMAT:** 4 Sound Filmstrips or 2 VHS Videotapes
(Videotapes are Filmstrip to Video Transfers)

CONTENTS:

"History" Students are introduced to the Dewey Decimal System through a look at nonfiction books that describe historical times and events.

"Science" More nonfiction books are introduced through a look at several books available in the science section of the LMC.

"Sports and Hobbies" Students take a look at the various subjects covered in the 700s section of the Dewey Decimal System. In addition, skills for using encyclopedias and almanacs are used.

"Art and Music" More books that can be found in the 700s are introduced through a look at the work of several artists and musicians. Use of audiovisual materials for finding information is introduced.

Teacher Guides Included

NOTES:

Although all the sections are not included, these filmstrips are wonderful for giving the students an overview of the most often used sections of the nonfiction books and their arrangement by subject area. The skills lessons are brief and subtle. The filmstrips are fairly short, about 12 minutes each, and allow time for extension of a lesson on the Dewey Decimal System. Although they are designed for students in grades 5 - 8, they can easily be used with fourth grade students and with more discussion, even third grade students.

PRODUCER: Pied Piper/AIMS Media   **PRICE:** Filmstrips, $120.00
9710 DeSoto Avenue   Videotapes, $125.00
Chatsworth, CA 91311-4409

TITLE: *Literature for Children, Series 6*   **FORMAT:** 4 Sound Filmstrips or 2 VHS Videotapes
(Videotapes are Filmstrip to Video Transfers)

CONTENTS:

"Mysteries" Students are introduced to several outstanding mystery books and become familiar with the elements that make a good mystery story.

"Epics and Legends" The special attributes of epics and legends and how they differ from other types of literature are discussed through the introduction of such legendary characters as Robin Hood and King Arthur.

"Realistic Fiction" Most students enjoy reading realistic fiction even though they don't really know that's what it's called. Several examples of realistic fiction are introduced, including Summer of the Swans.

"Science Fiction" The popular book, A Wrinkle in Time, is used to introduce students to books of fiction about the future.

Teacher Guides Included

NOTES:

This set of filmstrips is geared to students in grades 5 - 8 and some of the books selected to illustrate the genres are on a slightly higher reading level. This makes these filmstrips more useful in sixth grade although they can be used with fifth grade students and may inspire even fourth graders to venture into some more difficult reading.

PRODUCER: Pied Piper/AIMS Media   **PRICE:** Filmstrips, $120.00
9710 DeSoto Avenue   Videotapes, $125.00
Chatsworth, CA 91311-4409

TITLE: _Literature for Children, Series 7a_   **FORMAT:** 4 Sound Filmstrips or 2 VHS Videotapes
(Videotapes are Filmstrip to Video Transfers)

CONTENTS:

"Imagine That!" Picture books are used to introduce the kinds of books written from the author's imagination. The role of the library
media specialist is discussed briefly.

"Just Like Me" Students are introduced to picture books about feelings. The term _author_ is defined.

"Books about Real Things" Nonfiction books are introduced and the differences between _real_ and _make-believe_ are discussed. The
term _fiction_ is defined.

"Stories without Words" The importance of illustrations in picture books is discussed through the discussion of several wordless
picture books. The term _illustrator_ is defined.

Teacher Guides Included

NOTES:

This series of filmstrips is _just right_ for students in the first grade, although the programs can be used in second grade or
kindergarten. The picture books used to illustrate the concepts are of high quality and of interest to the students.

PRODUCER: Pied Piper/AIMS Media   **PRICE:** Filmstrips, $120.00
9710 DeSoto Avenue   Videotapes, $125.00
Chatsworth, CA 91311-4409

TITLE: _Literature for Children, Series 7b_   **FORMAT:** 4 Sound Filmstrips or 2 VHS Videotapes
(Videotapes are Filmstrip to Video Transfers)

CONTENTS:

"Animal Stories" The concept of _character_ is introduced to students through the discussion of several animal characters in familiar
picture books.

"What's So Funny?" The concept of _plot_ is discussed through the introduction of several humorous picture books.

"Exploring New Places" The concept of _setting_ is introduced though the use of picture books with settings in various parts of the
world.

"Stories about Friends" Familiar books about friends and friendships are used to encourage children to treat their books as friends.

Teacher Guides Included

NOTES:

These filmstrips are like _pre-recorded_ book talks. Their advantage is in the large size of the projected pictures and in the special
effects. The LMS can extend the lesson by reading one of the books introduced in the filmstrip.

PRODUCER: Pied Piper/AIMS Media   **PRICE:** Filmstrips, $120.00
9710 DeSoto Avenue   Videotapes, $125.00
Chatsworth, CA 91311-4409

TITLE: _Literature for Children, Series 7c_   **FORMAT:** 5 Sound Filmstrips or 2 VHS Videotapes
(Videotapes are Filmstrip to Video Transfers)

CONTENTS:

"Scary Stories" Several _scary_ books are introduced and the students become aware that picture books are arranged in alphabetical
order by the author's last name.

"Yummy Stories about Food" Humorous stories about food, such as <u>Cloudy with a Chance of Meatballs</u> are presented and the use
of the picture dictionary is introduced.

"Nature Poems and Stories" Books about nature and books with rhyme are introduced.

"Books about Pets" Several books about pets are presented and the concept of _easy reading_ books is introduced.

"By the Sea" The students experience vicarious adventures on a river and at the seashore through books about these topics. They
are also introduced to the magazine section of the LMC.

Teacher Guides Included

NOTES:

All three of these sets of filmstrips, <u>Literature for Children, Series 7a, 7b & 7c</u> are wonderful for use in the primary grades. They
are about the right length, about 11 minutes each and they use excellent picture books which excite the students about reading. The
vocabulary words and other concepts are presented in a subtle manner as part of the whole experience.

PRODUCER: Pied Piper/AIMS Media   **PRICE:** Filmstrips, $145.00
9710 DeSoto Avenue   Videotapes, $150.00
Chatsworth, CA 91311-4409

TITLE: *Literature for Children, Series 8*   **FORMAT:** 6 Sound Filmstrips or 3 VHS Videotapes
(Videotapes are Filmstrip to Video Transfers)

CONTENTS:

"Folktales Then and Now" The students are introduced to the origins of folktales as verbal stories handed down from one generation
      to another and from one culture to another.
"Folktale Characters" The concepts of *good* and *evil* are explored through folktale characters.
"Folktale Wisdom" The *moral of the story* is explored through a presentation of fables and fairy tales.
"Folktales from Afar" Several folktales from other counties are introduced as expressions of those cultures.
"Funny Folktales" Humorous and satirical folktales are presented.
"Magical World of Folktales" The timeless theme of using magical powers to avert tragedy is introduced through Native American,
      African and European folktales.
Teacher Guides Included

NOTES:

This set of filmstrips could be used in its entirety to present a unit on folktales. Unfortunately, there is usually not enough time for
such in-depth study. Instead, one or two of the filmstrips could be used to introduce folktales to students in grades 3 - 6.

PRODUCER: Pied Piper/AIMS Media   **PRICE:** Filmstrips, $190.00
               9710 DeSoto Avenue   Videotapes, $199.00
               Chatsworth, CA 91311-4409

TITLE: *Literature for Children, Series 9*   **FORMAT:** 5 Sound Filmstrips or 2 VHS Videotapes
(Videotapes are Filmstrip to Video Transfers)

CONTENTS:

"Character" Using characters from well-known children's books, the students are introduced to one of the four attributes of the story
      elements, *character*.
"Plot" Two well-loved children's books are used to illustrate the problem, action and climax of fictional writing.
"Setting" The concepts of *time* and *place* of a story are introduced through discussion of two outstanding children's books
"Style" The students are introduced to the writing styles of two authors of books for children.
"Theme" Students try to find the main idea of two well-known children's book.
Teacher Guides Included

NOTES:

Often lessons concerning these elements of fiction involve only discussion and worksheets. This set of filmstrips not only offers
excellent examples of the elements of fiction but introduces the students in grades 4 - 6 to some outstanding literature as well.

PRODUCER: Pied Piper/AIMS Media   Filmstrips, $175.00
               9710 DeSoto Avenue   **PRICE:** Videotapes, $190.00
               Chatsworth, CA 91311-4409

TITLE: *Literature to Enjoy & Write About, Series 1*   **FORMAT:** 5 Sound Filmstrips or 2 VHS Videotapes
(Videotapes are Filmstrip to Video Transfers)

CONTENTS:

"Diary-Journal" After experiencing several recent children books, the students can practice writing about their daily experiences.
"New Endings" Students are introduced to the adventure in <u>Hatchet</u> and <u>Julie of the Wolves</u> and are encouraged to think of different
      endings for books.
"Problem Solving" Students experience the fun of such humorous books as <u>Superfudge</u> and learn to look for more than one solution
      to a problem.
"Mapping" Students are introduced to the idea of story mapping and webbing through the use of several well-known mystery books.
"Interviewing" Students look at biographies to learn the technique of getting pertinent information and writing it down.
Teacher Guides Included

NOTES:

Even if these filmstrips are not used to promote creative writing experiences, the students will be introduced to some current and
outstanding books that they'll want to read for themselves.

PRODUCER: Pied Piper/AIMS Media   **PRICE:** Filmstrips, $175.00
               9710 DeSoto Avenue   Videotapes, $199.95
               Chatsworth, CA 91311-4409

TITLE: _Literature to Enjoy & Write About, Series 2_ **FORMAT:** 5 Sound Filmstrips or 2 VHS Videotapes
(Videotapes are Filmstrip to Video Transfers)

CONTENTS:

"Friendly Letter" Students write letters to book characters telling of their reactions to the events in the stories.

"Persuasive Writing" The importance of knowing your subject in persuasive writing is explained to students through an introduction
to several examples of children's nonfiction books.

"Book Review" Using basic story elements as criteria, students are given an opportunity to _rate_ several well-known children's books.
They then have an opportunity to create sequels to the stories.

"Sequel" After viewing two well-known children's animal stories, students are encouraged to write sequels to them.

"Reader's Theater" Students are able to take part in dramatizing parts of several exciting children's books.

Teacher Guides included

NOTES:

Students in grades 4 – 6 have an opportunity to become involved in the plots and characters of some great children's books. The
books used in this series of filmstrips will be checked out continuously as soon as these filmstrips are shown.

PRODUCER: Pied Piper/AIMS Media   **PRICE:** Filmstrips, $175.00
             9710 DeSoto Avenue   Videotapes, $199.95
             Chatsworth, CA 91311-4409

TITLE: _Library Manners for Primaries - 'Shh...Quiet Please'_   **FORMAT:** 1 Sound Filmstrip

CONTENTS:

Students are introduced to the various materials found in the library and to guidelines for taking care of those materials. Rules of
the library and reasons for following those rules are also discussed. The program presents an overview of the LMC for students
in the primary grades.

NOTES:

Although this filmstrip was made several years ago, its cartoon format makes it very useful today. It's a great introduction for a first
or second LMC visit for students in kindergarten and first grade.

PRODUCER: Eye Gate Media   **PRICE:** $39.00
             3333 Elston Avenue
             Chicago, IL 60618-5898

TITLE: _Hooray for the Library_   **FORMAT:** 4 Sound Filmstrips

CONTENTS:

"Magic Book" Students meet a magician who decides that his collection of magic books should be more organized when he turns
himself into a frog and then is unable to find the book needed to reverse the spell.

"Library to the Rescue" A little creature from outer space visits a library on Earth to try to find the answer to a perplexing question.

"Dog Who Wanted to Join the Library" A clever dog likes to read so much that he learns to write his name so he can get a library
card.

"How to Hunt for Dinosaurs" Students discover how to use the library to find both fiction and nonfiction books about dinosaurs.

Teacher Guides Included

NOTES:

This filmstrip set was produced in 1977, but its cartoon format and clever characters make it appealing for today's children. The
concepts are presented in a entertaining way that's great for students in first and second grades.

PRODUCER: Eye Gate Media   **PRICE:** Set of 4 Filmstrips, $109.00
             3333 Elston Avenue   Individual Filmstrips, $39.00
             Chicago, IL 60618-5898

TITLE: *Animated Video Reference Library*   **FORMAT:** 4 VHS Videotapes

CONTENTS:

"Animated Almanac" A lively *rap* introduces students to the kinds of information found in an almanac and demonstrates how to read and interpret that information.
"Animated Encyclopedia" The volumes of a set of encyclopedia *come alive* to show students how to research a subject in this invaluable reference tool.
"Animated Atlas" The different kinds of atlases are presented and students are instructed in finding and using information in them.
"Animated Dictionary" Use of the dictionary is reviewed and the thesaurus and specialized dictionaries are introduced.

Teacher Guides and Student Worksheets Included

NOTES:

Through the magic of claymation, these four basic reference books are able to *speak for themselves* in order to help fourth through sixth grade students who are struggling with research projects in the library. The programs are appealing and just the right length, an average of 18 minutes each. They offer basic information in an entertaining way.

PRODUCER: Society for Visual Education
1345 Diversey Parkway
Chicago, IL 60614–1299

PRICE: Set of 4 Videotapes, $265.00
Individual Videotapes, $79.00

TITLE: *Encyclopedia Brown's Information Skills Mysteries*   **FORMAT:** 4 Sound Filmstrips

CONTENTS:

"Case of the Divining Rod" Students are introduced to the Library Media Center, its basic arrangement and the many varied resources it contains.
"Case of the Explorers Money" Students are shown how to use card and computerized catalogs and are made aware of the important parts of a book.
"Case of the Balloon Man" The reference section and its various resources are explored.
"Case of the Cave Drawing" Students are instructed in the proper use of reference tools and are introduced to note-taking skills.

Teacher Guides and Student Worksheets Included

NOTES:

These programs make learning about the LMC seem like fun. They also show the resources being used for realistic purposes. They're *perfect* for fourth grade and can be used with other Encyclopedia Brown filmstrips to create an entire unit on the *Boy Detective*. In addition, they help renew the students' interest in the Encyclopedia Brown mystery books.

PRODUCER: Society for Visual Education
1345 Diversey Parkway
Chicago, IL 60614–1299

PRICE: Set of 4 Filmstrips, $175.00
Individual Filmstrips, $39.00

TITLE: *Ripley's® Library Research Skills*   **FORMAT:** 4 Sound Filmstrips or 1 VHS Videotape
(Videotape is Filmstrip to Video Transfer)

CONTENTS:

"Exploring the Library with Ripley's®" Students are introduced to libraries and the resources available there. The filmstrip includes an introduction to the Dewey Decimal System and the Library of Congress Classification System as well as an explanation of locating nonfiction books.
"Starting Your Research on Ripley's®" This program describes the use of the card catalog for finding books for research projects.
"Ripley's® Introduces Other Sources" Students are instructed in the uses of the atlas and the almanac.
"Confirming Your Ripley's® Research" Facts are taken from Ripley's Believe It or Not!®, and students see the step by step process for verifying them using the resources in the library.

Teacher Guides and Student Worksheets Included

NOTES:

The information is presented in a simple, straight-forward manner and is highlighted with interesting facts and trivia about books and libraries from Ripley's Believe It or Not!® A great program for fifth or sixth grades.

PRODUCER: Society for Visual Education
1345 Diversey Parkway
Chicago, IL 60614–1299

PRICE: Filmstrips, $175.00
Videotape, $175.00

TITLE: *Ripley's® Library Research Skills*   **FORMAT:**   2 Apple Computer Disks

CONTENTS:

Disk One, "Beginning Library Research Skills" Students move through Ripley's® Library identifying parts of catalog cards, labeling books as fiction, nonfiction or biography and determining the Dewey classification of books.

Disk Two, "Using Other Sources" Students work their way through the reference section answering questions about encyclopedias atlases and almanacs.

NOTES:

Based on Ripley's Believe It or Not!® these two disks are designed to accompany the set of filmstrips by the same name, but can definitely be used independently of the filmstrips. These programs are useful in a computer center. They are very simple to use and reinforce LMC skills for students in fourth through sixth grades.

PRODUCER: Society for Visual Education   **PRICE:**   With Filmstrips, $239.00
1345 Diversey Parkway   Computer Software Only, $84.00
Chicago, IL 60614–1299

TITLE: *School Library Adventures of the Lollipop Dragon®* **FORMAT:** 4 Sound Filmstrips or 1 VHS Videotape
(Videotape is Filmstrip to Video Transfer)

CONTENTS:

"Your School Library" Students are transported magically to the LMC and discover all the resources there.
"Finding What You Want" Students are introduced to LMC arrangement, LMC behavior and care of LMC materials.
"Parts of a Book" In addition to learning about the parts of a book, the students are instructed in the importance of alphabetical order, the arrangement of books on the shelves and the Dewey Decimal System.
"Using Audiovisual Material and Equipment" The various kinds of AV software and hardware, as well as their use and care, are introduced.
Teacher Guides and Student Worksheets included

NOTES:

Using the familiar character, Lollipop Dragon, this series of programs offers basic instruction in LMC skills and gives a thorough overview of the materials and services offered in the LMC. The program was made several years ago, but the cartoon format never goes out of style and the terminology is very current. The filmstrips last an average of 17 minutes each and are great for second and third grades.

PRODUCER: Society for Visual Education   **PRICE:**   Filmstrips, $175.00
1345 Diversey Parkway   Videotapes, $175.00
Chicago, IL 60614–1299

TITLE: *School Library Adventures of the Lollipop Dragon®*   **FORMAT:**   2 Apple Computer Disks

CONTENTS:

Disk One, "Exploring Library Land" Students practice alphabetizing and vocabulary skills.

Disk Two, "Library Treasure Hunt" Students move Lollipop Dragon through a LMC to locate and gather specific materials.

NOTES:

These computer programs are designed to accompany the filmstrip series of the same title, but they can be purchased and used independently of the filmstrips. Disk Two is especially fun once students *get the hang of it*. These computer programs are useful for students in third and fourth grades.

PRODUCER: Society for Visual Education   **PRICE:**   With Filmstrips, $239.00
1345 Diversey Parkway   Computer Software Only, $104.00
Chicago, IL 60614–1299

TITLE: *Check Out Your Library*   **FORMAT:** 3 VHS Videotapes

CONTENTS:

"Check Out Your Library: Reference" Students are introduced to the kinds of books found in the reference section and their use in the LMC.

"Check Out Your Library: Nonfiction" Students are introduced to the classes of the Dewey Decimal System that are used most often, including the biography section.

"Check Out Your Library: Fiction" Classic short stories and novels by the authors Mark Twain, Edgar Allen Poe, Jack London and Louisa May Alcott are presented to the students.

NOTES:

Using *rap* accompanied by music, these live action programs offer fifteen-minute overviews of the various sections of the LMC. Recommended for students in middle school, two of these programs are appropriate for upper elementary students as well. The program about *fiction* is geared more toward middle school, but it can be used with sixth grade to introduce the *classics*. The program about *nonfiction books* is very useful for students in grades 4 - 6 (and possibly third grade) even though all of the ten Dewey classes are not included. The *reference* program can be used with students in grades 4 - 6 and gives an excellent overview.

PRODUCER: Society for Visual Education
1345 Diversey Parkway
Chicago, IL 60614–1299

PRICE: Set of 4 Videotapes, $199.00
Individual Videotapes, $79.00

TITLE: *Encyclopedia Brown Introduces Report-Writing Skills*   **FORMAT:** 4 Sound Filmstrips

CONTENTS:

"Case of the Missing Statue" Students are introduced to the differences between fact and fiction and are instructed in topic selection for reports and in the importance of good note-taking skills.

"Case of the Happy Nephew" Students are shown how to use their notes to write an outline and how to identify the main topic and subtopic.

"Case of the Kidnapped Pigs" Guidelines for planning the report and writing a rough draft are given.

"Case of the Marble Shooter" Students are instructed in revising, proofreading and making the final report.

Teacher Guides and Student Worksheets included

NOTES:

These programs make report writing seem simple. After each skill is introduced, the *Boy Detective* tells about one of his interesting cases and gives the students a chance to solve it. Skills sheets, which are included, are designed to be used with the program but could be completed with the class after the filmstrips (which averages 12 1/2 minutes) are finished.

PRODUCER: Society for Visual Education
1345 Diversey Parkway
Chicago, IL 60614–1299

PRICE: Set of 4 Filmstrips, $175.00

TITLE: *Information Station*   **FORMAT:** 3 5.25" Apple Computer Disks
or 1 3.5" Apple Computer Disk

CONTENTS:

Students work at an imaginary satellite library of the future where they must use the LMC's resources to answer ecological questions from users around the world. In Level 1, the students are introduced, step-by-step, to finding information in reference books, the card catalog and periodicals. Level 2 is more difficult because some of the steps are eliminated and in Level 3, the students must decide the steps for doing the research independently.

Teacher Guide and Student Worksheets Included

NOTES:

Not only is this program challenging, it's also *timely*. Students are not only exposed to the use of research skills such as searching for information, taking notes and writing a report, they also glean some useful information for *saving the planet*! Students in grades 4 - 6 should really enjoy this program.

PRODUCER: Society for Visual Education
1345 Diversey Parkway
Chicago, IL 60614–1299

PRICE: $144.00

TITLE: _The Right Book for You_

FORMAT: 2 Sound Filmstrips or 1 VHS Videotape
(Videotape is Enhanced Filmstrip Transfer)

CONTENTS:

"Getting Started" Students are encouraged to find books that appeal to their interests rather than checking out books for book reports only. Practical guidelines are presented for getting around in the LMC to locate different kinds of books and various sources of information.

"Looking Further" The parts of a book are introduced in a practical and useful situation. The students can see how to use the index and the table of contents to make sure they have the books they need.

Teacher Guide Included

NOTES:

Students will relate to the character in this filmstrip and so will the LMS. Although these programs can be used with students in grades 4 - 6, the sixth grade students will benefit the most. The voice and tone of the narrator will catch their attention and leave them with some new thoughts on reading books and using the LMC.

PRODUCER: Cheshire, Dept. C
PO Box 61109
Denver, CO 80206

PRICE: Filmstrips, $69.95
Individual Videotapes, $74.95

TITLE: _Enjoying a Good Story_

FORMAT: 2 Sound Filmstrips or 1 VHS Videotape
(Videotape is Enhanced Filmstrip Transfer)

CONTENTS:

"The Story: A Time for No Unicorns" Students listen to a story about a wizard's search through time for a unicorn.

"Parts of the Story: A Closer Look" Students are introduced to the elements of fiction and their development in the previous story.

Teacher Guide Included

NOTES:

Students will enjoy the fantasy of the story presented in Part 1 and will be able to see how a story develops. This program is especially useful with sixth grade students because of the tone and mannerisms of the narrator.

PRODUCER: Cheshire, Dept. C
PO Box 61109
Denver, CO 80206

PRICE: Filmstrips, $69.95
Individual Videotapes, $74.95

TITLE: _How to Read a Good Book and Live to Tell about It_ **FORMAT:** 2 Sound Filmstrips or 1 VHS
Videotape
(Videotape is Enhanced Filmstrip Transfer)

CONTENTS:

"Getting the Most from Reading" Students are given guidelines for finding interesting books for their reports, for determining what information to seek and for taking notes on the information they've found.

"Sharing Your Ideas" Students are shown how to put their information into an outline and are given tips for making oral and written reports.

Teacher Guide Included

NOTES:

Students in grades 4 - 6 will relate to the situations presented in these filmstrips. The programs offer a humorous solution for the LMS or teacher to the introduction of book report assignments.

PRODUCER: Cheshire, Dept. C
PO Box 61109
Denver, CO 80206

PRICE: Filmstrips, $69.95
Individual Videotapes, $74.95

TITLE: *Tomes & Talismans*   **FORMAT:**   13 VHS Videotapes

CONTENTS:

Set far in the future when most humans have left and the earth is inhabited by an unintellectual, destructive race called the Wipers, this series of programs demonstrates the practical use of information skills. The one human left on earth, who just happens to be a librarian, is teamed with a group of teenaged *aliens,* the Users, who want to reclaim the planet for constructive purposes. In each of the programs they use the library to decipher clues from the *Universal Being* who helps them defeat the Wipers and *save the earth.*

Teacher Guide Included

NOTES:

This series of videotapes will hold the attention of fifth and sixth grade students for the full twenty minutes and when each episode is over, the students will ask for more. It's a great review of everything about a library media center. The programs are also available on the public broadcasting station.

PRODUCER: Great Plains National   **PRICE:** $432.00
P. O. Box 80609
Lincoln, Nebraska   68501

TITLE: *How to Use Children's Magazine Guide*   **FORMAT:**   1 Sound Filmstrip

CONTENTS:

Students doing research for reports demonstrate step–by–step instructions for using <u>Children's Magazine Guide</u> to find articles in various children's magazines.

Student Worksheet Included
Teacher Guide Included

NOTES:

This is such an outstanding filmstrip that the students can view it independently and be able to use the <u>Children's Magazine Guide</u> without any assistance. It is very useful for students in grades 4 – 6.

PRODUCER: R.R. Bowker   **PRICE:** $30.00
245 West 17th Street
New York, NY 10114–0418

TITLE: *Newbery Medal Winners*   **FORMAT:**   4 Sound Filmstrips or VHS Videotapes
(Videotapes are Filmstrip to Video Transfers)

CONTENTS:

Several of the popular books which have been awarded the Newbery Medal are presented through the use of short reviews made by kid, a librarian , teachers and a bookstore owner.

NOTES:

The format chosen to introduce these books is very appealing to students, especially the comments made by the students on the filmstrip. Students in fourth, fifth and sixth grade will be motivated to read more of the Newbery books.

PRODUCER: Library Filmstrip Center   **PRICE:**   Set of 4 Filmstrips, $188.00
205 E. Locust St.   Videotapes, $188.00
Bloomington, IL 61701

TITLE: *Caldecott Medal Winners*

FORMAT: 4 Sound Filmstrips or VHS Videotapes
(Videotapes are Filmstrip to Video Transfers)

CONTENTS:

Several of the popular books which have been awarded the Caldecott Medal are presented through the use of short reviews made by kids, a librarian, teachers and a bookstore owner.

NOTES:

The format chosen to introduce these books is very appealing to students and is a marvelous way to introduce them to many great picture books in a short amount of time.

PRODUCER: Library Filmstrip Center
205 E. Locust St.
Bloomington, IL 61701

PRICE: Set of 4 Filmstrips $188.00
Videotapes, $188.00

TITLE: *Meet the Newbery Author Series*

FORMAT: 1 Sound Filmstrip Each

CONTENTS:

Individual filmstrips introduce the author and the books by that author. Authors available:

Lloyd Alexander	William Armstrong	Natalie Babbitt
Carol Ryrie Brink	Betsy Byars	James Lincoln & Christopher Collier
Susan Cooper	Eleanor Estes	Russell Freeman
Jean Craighead George	Bette Greene	Virginia Hamilton
Madeleine L'Engle	Arnold Lobel	Scott O'Dell
Katherine Paterson	Isaac Bashevis Singer	Mildred D. Taylor
Nancy Willard	Laura Ingalls Wilder	Laurence Yep

NOTES:

In addition to these sound filmstrips, many new titles and series about various authors are being produced on live action videotape. Check the producer's catalog for additional titles.

PRODUCER: American School Publishers
SRA School Group
155 North Wacker Drive
Chicago, IL 60606

PRICE: $47.00 Each

TITLE: *Randolph Caldecott:*
the Man Behind the Medal

FORMAT: 1 Sound Filmstrip or 1 VHS Videocassette

CONTENTS:

The life of this talented English illustrator is depicted through selections of his drawings and how they were influenced by the Victorian Era of his time.

NOTES:

This fifteen–minute filmstrip is informative and interesting to the students. It should be included in any unit about the Caldecott Medal.

PRODUCER: Weston Woods
Weston, CT 06833–1199

PRICE: Filmstrip, $35.00
Videotape, $39.00

INDEX

Dr. Catharyn Roach is Library Media Specialist at the Dan D. Rogers Elementary School in the Dallas Independent School District. She has worked in school library media centers for the past 17 years.

Dr. JoAnne Moore is Director of Library Media Programs and Services in the Dallas Independent School District and an adjunct professor in the School of Library and Information Science at Texas Woman's University. She serves on the advisory board for the School of Library and Information Science at the University of North Texas and the Library Service Council for Texas State Library. She was recently elected as representative-at-large for the Texas Library Association.

Dr. Barbara L. Stein is Associate Professor at the School of Library and Information Science at the University of North Texas. She has experience both as a school teacher and a media specialist.

Cover design: Apicella Design
Typography: C. Roberts